INDIANS
OF THE
CHICAGO
AREA

2nd Edition

Compiled and Edited by Terry Straus

312-741-5000

Library of Congress Catalog Card Number 90-63111
ISBN 0-944898-03-3

Research for this book was funded by the NALCO Foundation.

Cover design by Henrietta Crandall

Foreword

This collection of writings about Indians in the Chicago area includes several interesting perspectives and diverse points of view. Each writer brings a special contribution to understanding the history of the region. Some are non-Indians whose recording and interpretation of the Indian experience comes largely from research. Others are Indians who have blended historical documentation about Indians with their own experiences. All of these writings are of equal value in understanding American Indian activity in the Chicago area.

However, too few Indians, especially those whose commitment is to tribe and community, have had the opportunity to study, analyze, and write about their own history and experience. The NAES College Press, publisher of this book, is established to provide a forum for the articulation of Indian views and will contribute to alleviating this problem.

For those non-Indians who have contributed to these writings, we are appreciative. At the same time, we challenge them to encourage, train, and make a place for new Indian scholars and writers. The challenge to Indians in Chicago and other communities, especially but not exclusively where NAES has campuses, is much more difficult to realize; that is, careful attention is necessary to assure our place among the predominant students and writers about American Indians.

Faith Smith, President
NAES College
1990

TABLE OF CONTENTS

7. BIBLIOGRAPHIC ESSAY

INTRODUCTION

Terry Straus
NAES College

This volume began in a history seminar at the Chicago campus of NAES (Native American Educational Services) College. Seminar participants—students, faculty, and guests—have all contributed to it. In addition, Virgil Vogel generously agreed to provide an historical overview and various biographical sketches. While David Beck [*The Chicago American Indian Community, 1893-1988* (Chicago: NAES College Press, 1988)] has clearly established the range of published material on the Chicago American Indian Community since 1893, this volume covers a greater time span and is the first comprehensive resource for the general reader. Papers included represent the special interests of seminar participants but, in response to the many requests NAES has received, they have been written with Chicago area school teachers specially in mind.

In spite of its winds, sand and marshes, the Chicago area has been almost continuously inhabited by Native American people for hundreds of years. The Potawatomis ceded the last of their land in the 1833 treaty of Chicago (Wiese, Red Cloud, Straus, Red Cloud, and Harris), but Native American people of various tribes remained in the area, a few on individual grants of land. Streets of the city followed old Indian trails (Vogel; Catches, Straus and Anderson) and numerous landmarks (Lloyd) serve to remind contemporary residents that the city has a history considerably longer than the 150 years it recently celebrated.

The present Chicago American Indian community includes some sixteen thousand members from more than sixty different tribes (Beck; Beck and LaPier). There is a lot of movement into and out of the area by Native American people, just as there has been throughout the centuries (Tanner). The greatest influx, however, came as a result of the federal relocation program (Fixico) in which Chicago served as one of two main relocation centers. Native American communities have always included minority populations, and early village life in the Great Lakes was characterized by a dynamic inter-tribal mix (Tanner). Chicago itself has long been a "cosmopolitan community" (Miller) and Native American people in Chicago have retained tribal identity, relationship to home reservations, and respect for tribal traditions (NAES class paper).

2. HISTORICAL OVERVIEW

The Tribes
Virgil Vogel

The Tribes

Virgil Vogel

About twelve thousand years ago the glacial ice that covered northern Illinois began to retreat northward. The ice gouged out the basin
of Lake Michigan and the rivers that flow into it or toward the Mississippi. The heaps of rock and other debris which it left behind,
called moraine, can be seen today in the hills which arise here and
there from the flat prairies.

As the ice melted, bands of people moved into the region, camping
and hunting along the streams. No one knows what language they
spoke or from which direction they came. Many believe they were
descendants of Asian tribes who crossed the then-existing land bridge
across Bering Strait to Alaska more than 25,000 years ago. They
spread southward over many years to all parts of the American conti-
nents. Columbus called those early Americans whom he encountered
in the West Indies in 1492 "Indians" because he believed he had
landed in the East Indies.

By the time of European entry into America, complex and
advanced social systems had been developed by the mound builders of
the Mississippi valley and by other native peoples in parts of Central
and South America. In the latter places agriculture began in America
and many domesticated crops were developed which eventually added
much to the world's food supply. Many of these plants spread to
North America and became an important part of the food supply in
our region of the country. By far the most important crop was maize,
or "Indian corn," which remains today the leading crop grown in the
United States. The Indians of the Northeastern woodlands and others
also grew beans, pumpkins, squash, sunflowers, and tobacco.

We do not know a great deal about the earliest inhabitants of our
region. They had no system of writing and so left no records. What
we do know about them is based on the artifacts uncovered by archae-
ologists. From village sites and ancient burials they have found stone
implements, weapons, tools, jewelry and other ornaments, and pottery.

When white people first penetrated the region of the Great Lakes
in the 1600s, they found the area widely though thinly populated, in
most places, by numerous tribes of Indians. They had communal
social systems and democratic political structures in which power
rested with the people. Chiefs were chosen for their distinction and
service to the tribe. They served but did not command, and were subject to removal. Women did much menial work, to free their men for

hunting and defense, but they were not considered inferior. They enjoyed high social status. In many tribes they had sole authority over the children and dwellings. Ancestry was most commonly traced through the female or matrilineal line.

In those times great herds of buffalo roamed in Illinois, and they were hunted by the Indians armed with spears and bows and arrows. Deer, elk, bear, cougars, wildcats and smaller animals were also hunted for food and for hides. Wild turkeys, geese, and ducks also contributed to the Indian food supply. They foraged for wild plants and berries, but they were also farmers. Crops were planted by the women, and from the Indians the white pioneers borrowed important food crops.

They lived in wigwams which were usually dome-shaped dwellings consisting of a framework of saplings covered with woven rush mats in winter or elm bark in summer. Rectangular communal dwellings were also erected in permanent villages. They travelled mainly by land, and invented snowshoes and toboggans to facilitate travel in winter, when they did most of their hunting. They had no horses until these animals were introduced by the Spanish, first on the southern plains, from whence they gradually spread to the north and east. When they took to the water, they used dugout canoes. Their clothing and moccasins were of deerskin, ornamented with dyed porcupine quills, shell beads, elks' teeth, strips of fur, and bear claws. They wove bags from basswood fiber and made baskets and simple pottery. Some of their important food gathering activities were seasonal. The villages were nearly deserted while the Indians went on a winter hunt to far away places. There was a shorter summer hunt. One of the festive occasions was maple sugar time, which began in early March, as the sap began to rise. The sap was collected in bark boxes called mococks, which were attached to the trees below incisions that were made. Then it was boiled down to make syrup, and further boiled to make sugar. Sometimes earthen pots were used, and sometimes tightly woven baskets. The latter could be used for cooking by filling them with water and dropping hot stones into them until the water began to boil.

All of the Indian tribes that lived in this vicinity, except the Winnebago, spoke a language belonging to the Algonquian family, from which we have borrowed many place names as well as many words, including hickory, hominy, moose, opossum, papoose, pecan, raccoon, skunk, and squaw.

Our detailed knowledge of the Indians of the Chicago region begins with written accounts of the early white explorers. The first of these was Father Jacques Marquette, a Jesuit priest, from the mission of St. Ignace, in upper Michigan. In the early summer of 1673, with

Louis Joliet and five Frenchmen, he travelled by canoe via Green Bay and the Fox-Wisconsin waterway to the Mississippi, then turned south. On June 25 he reached the mouth of what is thought by some to be the Des Moines River, where he found an Indian village of three hundred cabins. The people were, said Marquette, members of the "peouarea" tribe of the Illinois (from Illiniwek, "people"). Their language was similar to that of the "allegonquin," so that they could be understood. He considered them of a "gentle and tractable disposition," and remarked upon the warmth of their reception. He said that they planted corn, beans, "melons," and squashes.

A few days later Marquette's party continued down the river to northeastern Arkansas, where they encountered the Michigamea, the most distant tribe of the Illinois confederacy, whose language was not intelligible. Soon thereafter, on July 17, Marquette's party began their return journey, entering and ascending the Illinois River near present Alton. Upriver, near present Starved Rock, he encountered a village of seventy-four cabins inhabited by another Illinois tribe, the Kaskaskia. He was well received here, and promised to return later to instruct them. One of their chiefs escorted his party to the Chicago portage, by which Marquette reached Green Bay in late September.

The next year, in late October, 1674, Marquette and his companions began a return trip to Illinois, following the western shore of Lake Michigan by canoe. Because of inclement weather and the priest's attack of dysentery, they did not reach the site of Chicago until early December. Although they were then only a hundred miles from the Kaskaskia, they found it necessary to winter there. On March 29 they set out again and reached the Indians eleven days later, during Easter week. There he preached to large crowds, but after a few days his weakness compelled him to begin his last voyage home. Returning by way of the Kankakee and the east shore of Lake Michigan, he died and was buried near the site of Ludington, Michigan.

Marquette's accounts give us our first meager information on the Illinois Indians. The next French visitor, Robert Rene Cavalier, Sieur de La Salle, arrived at the Starved Rock village in January, 1680, but found it deserted. He found the Indians at Lake Pimitoui (present Peoria) and after securing their friendship, built Fort Crevecoeur. Soon after, he returned to Canada, leaving his aide, Henri de Tonti, in charge. Most of the Frenchmen then pillaged the fort and deserted it. Only three French workmen and two missionaries remained with Tonti.

In September a war party of six hundred Iroquois appeared. One zealous warrior stabbed Tonti, but not too seriously, for Tonti succeeded in negotiating a truce. Meanwhile he advised the Illinois to

escape down river. After a few days, Tonti's diplomatic skills persuaded the Iroquois to leave. Soon after, he began construction of Fort
St. Louis on Starved Rock, finishing it in 1683.

La Salle aimed to build a commercial empire based on the fur
trade, and for that purpose, persuaded some three thousand Indians,
Illinois, Miami, and Shawnee, to settle near "Le Rocher." Apparently
La Salle saw some value in promoting tension between the Illinois
and Iroquois. Their war, he thought, might be settled "if there were
not cause to fear that, being at peace with the Iroquois and feeling
secure from their direction, the Illinois might wish to make war
against the Ottawa . . . and thus interrupt our commerce. But so long
as it can be contrived to keep them dependent upon us, they may
readily be held to their duty, and through them the more distant
nations by whom they are feared."

Indeed they became dependent, as Iroquois invasions and French
guile concentrated them first at "the Rock," then Lake Peoria, and
after 1700 in the vicinity of the small French settlements at Kaskaskia, Cahokia, and Prairie du Rocher, which grew up in the "American
Bottom," near present East St. Louis. In that area the remaining
tribes of Illinois, the Cahokia, Tamaroa, and Moingwena, preceded
the Kaskaskia, Peoria, and Michigamea. Here their numbers shrank
as they became more Europeanized. In 1750 Father Louis Vivier
wrote, "when the first missionaries came among the Illinois, we see,
by the writings they have left us, that they counted five thousand persons of all ages in that nation. Today we count but two thousand."
Alcohol, introduced diseases, and war, including attacks upon them
from northern Indians to avenge the murder of the Ottawa chief Pontiac by an Illinois in 1769, brought their numbers down to 150 when
their last remnant was moved to Kansas in 1833.

Before their nationhood was eroded, the Illinois and their lifeways
were described by Pierre de Liette, nephew of Tonti: "You can see no
finer looking people," he wrote. "They have legs that seem drawn with
an artist's pen. They carry their load of wood gracefully, with a proud
gait as finely as the best dancer .... they are full of life but at the same
time lazy." His other observations undermine the charge of laziness.
He described a buffalo hunt in which the Indians killed twelve hundred of the "wild cattle." Drying preserved the meat, and every part of
the animal was used. Moreover, the Indians grew large crops of
"watermelons," pumpkins and corn, and stored wild fruits, nuts, and
roots.

The egalitarianism of the Illinois contrasted so sharply with elitist
French customs that Father Vivier declared: "As there is neither rank
nor dignity among them, all men seem equal to them. An Illinois
would speak as boldly to the King of France as to the lowest of his

subjects .... They all live in great peace, which is due, in great measure, to the fact that each one is allowed to do what he pleases."

As the dwindling Illinois retreated southward, other tribes poured in, mainly from Wisconsin. First among them were the Miami, an Algonquian tribe, some of whom settled at the unoccupied site of Chicago about 1695. Then in 1696 the mission of the Guardian Angel was built among them by the Jesuit Father Francois Pinet. In 1698 a visitor, Father Jean de St. Cosme, reported that "the village of the Savages contains over a hundred and fifty cabins, and a league up the river is still another village almost as large." De Liette called Chicago "the most considerable village of the Miami." Before the century ended, and Pinet's mission closed, other Miami were spread along the Wabash River and its tributaries, as well as on the Maumee and St. Joseph Rivers in Ohio and Michigan, respectively. Their residence in Illinois was brief, but it may be from them that the name of our greatest metropolis was derived. On September 25, 1687, Henri Joutel, a survivor of La Salle's disastrous expedition to Texas during the previous year, wrote in his journal: "... we arrived at a place called Chicago which, according to what we could learn, has taken this name from the quantity of garlic which grows in this district, in the woods."

Next the Mascouten and Kickapoo descended from Wisconsin into central Illinois, where the Mascouten were apparently absorbed by the Kickapoo. The Kickapoo did not settle near Chicago, and their influence elsewhere was slight. Some of their villages were near Peoria and Danville. Their former presence is noted by the preservation of their name on a village and township, as well as several creeks and other features. The last of the Kickapoo were removed to Missouri, and thence to Kansas and Oklahoma, beginning in 1833. Their most distinguished individual leader was the prophet Kennekuk, the leader of a native religious revival.

The Foxes or Mesquakie ("red earth"), moving southward from the Green Bay region, were in Illinois before 1730. Unpopular with neighboring Algonquian speaking tribes because of their ties to the Iroquois, the Foxes were nearly decimated by a French and Indian force in September, 1730. The fugitives fled to the friendly Sauk, forming a dual alliance which was to endure for a century. Their last settlements in the state were at the present site of Rock Island and vicinity.

The only non-Algonquian tribe to live in Illinois in historic times were the Winnebago, who were Siouan speakers. They had peacefully resided for a long time with their Algonquian neighbors about Green Bay, Lake Winnebago, and along the Fox and Wisconsin Rivers, in Wisconsin. Only a few of them settled in Illinois, mainly in the Rockford area and along Rock River as far as Prophetstown. At that place their village headed by the prophet Wabokieshiek, an ally of the Sauk chief Black Hawk, was burned by state militia on May 10, 1832. By that time another band of Winnebago, led by Winneshiek, had already retreated to Wisconsin.

By far the most influential tribe to occupy the region about Chicago and northern Illinois was the Potawatomi. The earliest report of them is from Father Claude Allouez, who met them at Chequamegon on Lake Superior in 1666. Father Marquette found them near Sturgeon Bay, Wisconsin, in 1679, and La Salle met them on Green Bay five years later. They were closely allied to the Ojibwa, or Chippewa, and Ottawa tribes. These three were known as the "Three Fires," suggesting a loose confederacy stemming perhaps from an earlier time when they were one tribe. The name of the Potawatomi signifies "keepers of the fire." They had been much influenced by the French explorers and missionaries by the time they began drifting southward some time before 1750. They settled along the Lake Michigan shore from Milwaukee to Chicago, westward to Lake Geneva and Rock River, and southward to Peoria. They had settlements along the Fox River of Illinois and along the Kankakee. They moved into northern Indiana, occupying the region as far south as the Wabash, where the Miami lived, and into southern Michigan. In Michigan their main settlement was about present St. Joseph, but they reached up the lake shore to Grand River and eastward to the environs of Detroit. They continued to occupy these regions until the 1830s, when they were displaced by a series of treaties. The treaty signed at Chicago on September 26, 1833, provided for the removal of all Potawatomi from Illinois within two years. Several treaties with individual Potawatomi bands of Indiana and Michigan provided for the removal of some as late as 1838, though the last removal was from southwest Michigan in 1840. A few members of Pokagon's band and others remained in Michigan by special provisions. The exiled Indians were transported to southwestern Iowa, northwestern Missouri, and eastern Kansas.

Throughout the 1700s, the region west of Ft. Pitt (Pittsburgh) was peopled only by Indians and a few hundred French settlers huddled around the forts. France maintained a shadowy claim to all lands drained by the Great Lakes and the Mississippi. The French had cordial relations with most Indians in the region, intermarrying with them and converting many to the Catholic faith. The French and Indian War, 1754-1763, brought shattering changes, as the British ousted France from North America.

The Indians held themselves sovereign over the territory traded away by the diplomats at Paris. The Ottawa chief Pontiac, brooding over native grievances, forged an alliance of tribes reaching from the Seneca of western New York to the Sauks on the Mississippi.

In western Pennsylvania, wrote Francis Parkman in his lurid *Conspiracy of Pontiac*, "Before many hours elapsed, the night was lighted up by the glare of blazing dwellings, and the forest rang with the shrieks of the murdered inmates." The massacres long endured by the Indians drew little notice from historians of the nineteenth century.

Within six weeks of the beginning of the revolt on May 8, 1763, eight British posts fell to the Indians. Only Ft. Pitt and Detroit survived Indian attacks. To buy peace, the Royal Proclamation of October 7, 1763, forbade white settlement west of the sources of the streams that fell into the sea. George Croghan, a frontier diplomat, secured a truce, followed by a peace conference at Detroit, August 17, 1765. The peace created a grievance related to the American Revolution only ten years off. Settlers and speculators alike objected to their exclusion from the Indian country, and plotted to evade the royal edict.

Upon the outbreak of the American Revolution in 1775, Indian allegiance was divided. On the very eve of Lexington and Concord, frontier violence against Indians in Ohio led to Lord Dunmore's War (1774) which resulted in Indian defeat. The Ohio Shawnee, smarting from their setback, joined most of the Iroquois in support of the king. However, when George Rogers Clark's Virginia militia captured the British forts at Vincennes and Kaskaskia, in the summer of 1778, Clark called midwestern Indians to council at Cahokia. From as far as Milwaukee the Indians came, and a shaky alliance was forged, without which Clark could not have maintained his position in Illinois, nor recovered Vincennes after the British Colonel Hamilton recaptured it in December.

As the war ended, the Americans had the mistaken notion that British capitulation included the Indians, although the treaty ignored them. The tribes of the old Northwest, led by the Shawnee and Miami, fought to hold the Ohio River as a boundary against white settlement, and in 1790-91, led by Little Turtle of the Miami, they inflicted catastrophic defeats upon invading armies led by generals Josiah Harmar and Arthur St. Clair. It was a debacle worse than Custer's in 1876, costing six hundred American lives in the second incident alone. However, three years later, Mad Anthony Wayne crushed Indian defenders at Fallen Timbers, near present Toledo, while the nearby British denied them aid or sanctuary. Following the Jay treaty later that year between Britain and America, chiefs and warriors of twelve tribes signed the treaty of Greenville with Wayne, August 3, 1795. By its terms the Indians were compelled to cede southern Ohio and sixteen enclaves at strategic locations, among which was "One piece of land six miles square at Chikago river, emptying into the south- west end of Lake Michigan." Thus was obtained title to the site of the future metropolis, where Fort Dearborn would be built in 1803.

At Greenville the dike was breached and the way was opened for the white flood. More chunks of land were soon demanded, until resistance was stiffened by the Shawnee chief, Tecumseh, and his brother, the Prophet. They planned no aggression, but instead preached a return to the old ways and refusal to sell land, which was viewed as belonging collectively to all the Indians. Indiana governor William Henry Harrison, apparently intent on ending this impertinence, marched on Tecumseh's village at the junction of the Tippecanoe and Wabash Rivers, above present Lafayette, Indiana, at the head of nearly a thousand militia. Tecumseh, who travelled much to spread his message, was absent among the Creeks, but before dawn on November 7, 1812, the Prophet directed a preemptive attack on the encamped troops. Harrison's men repelled the Indians, burned the village, and destroyed the corn and livestock. The fame of this affair made Harrison president in 1840, but it turned the Indians of the region at once into bitter enemies on the eve of war between Great Britain and the United States.

When James Madison's war message was debated in Congress in June, 1812, the war hawks alleged that British-inspired Indian attacks required the conquest of Canada. The frustrated Indians, neglected by the British since 1795, were now showered with gifts and encouraged to fight. Capt. Nathan Heald, commander of the isolated garrison at Chicago's Fort Dearborn, was ordered by Gen. William Hull at Detroit to retreat to Fort Wayne. The sixty- eight-man garrison, including a dozen militia and a train of civilians with a wagonload of children, flanked by an escort of thirty mounted Miami led by Capt. William Wells, abandoned the fort on the morning of August 15, 1812. They had marched only two miles along the lake before they were confronted by five hundred Potawatomi and Ottawa warriors, led by the Ottawa warrior Blackbird. Heald attacked, and in fifteen minutes fifty-three whites died, including two women and twelve children. Black Partridge, a Potawatomi, saved the life of Mrs. Margaret Helm, wife of the second in command, vainly tried to rescue Capt. Wells, and protected some survivors afterward. Black Partridge had, the day before, returned to Heald the president's peace medal because of his inability to control the braves. His gallantry, however, failed to deter Gov. Ninian Edwards from utterly destroying his village near Peoria a few months later.

The family of John Kinzie, and Capt. Heald and his wife, both wounded, were sheltered at St. Joseph, Michigan, by Chief Topenebee and twenty-three-year-old Alexander Robinson (Che-Che-Pinqua). In the fall of 1812, to protect Heald from recapture by hostile Indians,

Robinson and his wife Catherine bundled the Healds into a bark canoe and paddled three hundred miles up the stormy lake shore to deliver them to the safety of British custody at Mackinac.

The war ended with the treaty of Ghent, which required the United States to restore to the tribes "all the possessions, rights, and privileges which they may have enjoyed" before the war. So it happened, during 1815, that the United States signed fourteen treaties with Indian tribes, not one of which contained land cessions or punitive clauses.

But plundering tactics were soon renewed. In 1816 the Potawatomi were pressured into ceding, for about 2 cents an acre, a tract twenty miles wide reaching from Lake Michigan to the Illinois River. In the next two decades the Potawatomi were intimidated, bribed, and intoxicated into signing two dozen more treaties which would deprive them of the last foot of land they possessed, excepting reserves to a few individuals, and exile them to Iowa, Missouri and Kansas. The final doom of Indian tenure in our region was assured by the inauguration in 1829 of President Andrew Jackson, who relentlessly pursued the goal of Indian dispossession. With other tribes preceding them, the last Potawatomi were removed from Illinois in 1835, and from Indiana in 1838. Chief Menominee of Twin Lakes, Indiana, tearfully pleaded that he had signed no removal treaty, but troops tied up the recalcitrants, and prodded them westward with bayonets. Descendants of these Indians live today on a reservation near Mayetta, Kansas, and on allotted lands in Shawnee County, Oklahoma. Some Potawatomi eluded exile by fleeing to northern Wisconsin. Their descendants live on reservations in Forest County, Wisconsin, and in Menominee County, Michigan.

Of all Midwest tribes, only the Sauk and some Foxes resisted expulsion, in 1832, during a brief flare-up known to history as the Black Hawk War. In 1804, by duplicitous means, Indiana territorial governor Harrison extracted from Quashquame a treaty ceding all Sauk and Fox lands in Illinois, in exchange for land in Iowa. However, they could live on the land until the government should require it. In 1831 the government at last compelled the Indians to cross the Mississippi, leaving their unharvested cornfields behind.

After a hungry winter in Iowa, Black Hawk (1767-1838), a subordinate Sauk chief, recrossed the Mississippi on April 5, 1832, at the mouth of Iowa River, at the head of nine hundred followers. They passed up their old village of Saukenuk at the mouth of the Rock, and ascended the river to join their Winnebago ally, Wabokieshiek, at Prophetstown. Black Hawk insisted he had no hostile intention, but merely wished to plant corn. However, war broke out when an undisciplined band of militia from Dixon, Illinois, fired on Black Hawk's truce party, bearing a white flag, on April 14, killing two. The three others raced back to Black Hawk's band of fifty warriors waiting at the site of the present village of Stillman Valley. The two hundred pursuing militia ran into an Indian ambush and twelve were killed, in the first skirmish of a three-month struggle.

The Sauks were unable to win the support of the Potawatomi or other tribes, although a small band of Potawatomi, with grievances of their own, attacked and killed fifteen people at the William Davis farm in La Salle County. Shabbona, long a friend of the whites, had warned the settlers to flee from that place, but they declined. The Potawatomi at Chicago, under the influence of Alexander Robinson and Billy Caldwell, remained neutral, and the militant young braves were confined in a camp on the Des Plaines River. A group of seventeen Kickapoo supporters of Black Hawk were killed in an encounter with Wisconsin volunteers under Col. Henry Dodge, near Woodford, Wisconsin, on June 16, 1832.

The Sauks, after engagements near Polo, Elizabeth, and Kellogg's Grove, in Illinois, retreated up Rock River to Lake Koshkonong, Wisconsin. Meanwhile, federal troops arrived, some of whom, under Gen. W. D. Henry, joined with Col. Dodge's volunteers. On July 21 they caught up with the Indians at Wisconsin Heights, just south of present Sauk City, where the beleaguered Indians held a much larger white force at bay while their women and children crossed the Wisconsin River on rafts.

Troops pursued the hungry and exhausted Indians to the banks of the Mississippi five miles below the mouth of the Bad Axe. There on August 1st the troops fired relentlessly on the Indians while a gunboat shelled them from the river. Some who swam across the river were killed by the Sioux on the other side. Black Hawk himself with a few followers escaped, but surrendered a few weeks later at Prairie du Chien. He was imprisoned for the winter at Jefferson Barracks, Missouri, then taken to Washington, where he met Jackson, and was finally returned to Iowa to live in the custody of the pliable Keokuk.

Meanwhile on September 21, the Treaty of Fort Armstrong extracted from the Indians a strip of their Iowa lands, as a penalty for the war. Finally, in 1845, they were, in consequence of another treaty, removed to Kansas. From there in 1867 they were again removed to Indian Territory, now Oklahoma, where their descendants remain. However, in the 1850s a party of Foxes returned to Iowa, where, with the consent of the governor and the support of sympathetic whites, they used treaty money to repurchase some land along Iowa River in Tama county, where their descendants now live.

Though expelled from the state which bears the name of Illinois, the Indians left their mark on its surface. The names of our map ring out hundreds of their colorful place names, and the corn tassels waving in the summer breeze throughout the state call attention to one of the great gifts of the first inhabitants. We built roads and railways along their ancient trails and dug canals along their portage paths. We adopted hundreds of their herbal medicines. Some of our youth organizations promote Indian lore in their programs. But beneath the superficial borrowing, the essence of Indian existence, a society in harmony with itself and with nature, and a cooperative social-economic life joined with individualism in personal and political matters, has vanished from non-Indian experience.

For Further Reading

Burt Anson, *The Miami Indians* (Norman: University of Oklahoma Press, 1970).

Hiram W. Beckwith, *The Illinois and Indiana Indians*. (New York: Arno Press, 1975). Reprint.

Elaine Bluhm, ed. *Indian Mounds and Villages in Illinois*. Bulletin No. 2, Illinois Archaeological Survey. Urbana: 1960.

_____ *Chicago Area Archaeology*. Bulletin No. 3, Illinois Archaeological Survey. Urbana: 1961.

Bureau of Indian Affairs. *Indians of the Great Lakes Region*. Washington: Government Printing Office, 1966.

John Dean Caton, *The Last of the Illinois and a Sketch of the Potawatomies*. (Chicago: Fergus Printing Co., 1876).

James A. Clifton, *The Prairie People*. (Lawrence: Regents Press of Kansas, 1977).

Thorne Deuel, "The First Americans: Prehistoric Indians of Illinois." *Illinois History*, November, 1959, pp. 27-29. For high schoolers.

_____, *American Indian Ways of Life*. Springfield: Illinois State Museum, 1958.

R. David Edmunds, *The Potawatomis*. (Norman: University of Oklahoma Press, 1978).

Clark Foreman, *The Last Trek of the Indians*. (Chicago: University of

Chicago Press, 1946).

A.M. Gibson, *The Kickapoos*. (Norman: University of Oklahoma Press, 1963).

Frank R. Grover, *Father Pierre Francois Pinet and his Mission of the Guardian Angel at Chicago, A.D. 1696-99*. (Chicago: 1907).

William T. Hagan, *The Sac and Fox Indians*. (Norman: University of Oklahoma Press, 1958).

Elijah Haines, *The American Indian*. (Evansville, Ind.: Unigraphic Corporation, 1979). Reprint.

"Indians Who Lived in Illinois." *Illinois History*. November, 1959, entire issue. For high schoolers.

"Indians Who Lived in Illinois." *Illinois History*. November, 1970, entire issue. For high schoolers.

"Indians in Illinois." *Illinois History*. November, 1975, entire issue. For high schoolers.

George P. Jensen, *Historic Chicago Sites*. (Chicago: Creative Enterprises, 1953).

Louise P. Kellogg, *Early Narratives of the Northwest, 1634-1699*. (New York: Charles Scribner's, 1917).

W. Vernon Kinietz, *The Indians of the Western Great Lakes, 1615-1760*. (Ann Arbor: University of Michigan Press, 1965).

Mrs. John H. Kinzie, *Wau-Bun: The Early Day in the Northwest*. (Chicago: Rand McNally Co., 1901).

Milo M. Quaife, *Chicago and the Old Northwest, 1673-1835*. (Chicago: University of Chicago Press, 1913).

_____, *The Development of Chicago, 1674-1914*. (Chicago: The Caxton Club, 1916).

_____, *Checagou: from Indian Wigwam to Modern City, 1673-1835*. (Chicago: University of Chicago Press, 1933).

_____, *The Western Country in the 17th Century*. (Now York: The Citadel Press, 1962).

_____, *Chicago's Highways Old and New: From Indian Trail to Motor Road*. (Ann Arbor: University Microfilms, 1968). Reprint.

James Scott, *The Illinois Nation.* 2 Parts. (Streator: Streator Historical Society, 1973, 1976).

Harry W. Spooner, *Indians of Northern Illinois.* (Tiskilwa, Illinois: Tiskilwa Chief, 1941).

William Duncan Strong, *Indian Tribes of the Chicago Region, with Special Reference to the Illinois and Potawatomi.* (Chicago: Field Museum, 1938).

John R. Swanton, *The Indian Tribes of North America.* Bulletin 145, Bureau of American Ethnology. (Washington: Government Printing Office, 1952).

Wayne C. Temple, *Indian Villages of the Illinois Country: Historic Tribes.* (Springfield: Illinois State Museum, 1958).

Virgil J. Vogel, *Indian Place Names in Illinois.* (Springfield: Illinois State Historical Society, 1963).

Otho Winger, *The Potawatomi Indians.* (Elgin, Illinois: Elgin Press, 1939).

Charles S. Winslow, *Indians of the Chicago Region.* 2d ed. (Chicago: the author, 1946). Juvenile.

Miriam Wood, Roberta Cramer and Emma Neve. *Indians of Early Chicago.* (Chicago: Chicago Museum of Natural History, 1957). Juvenile.

3. PEOPLE

Tribal Mixtures in Chicago Area Indian Villages

Helen Hornbeck Tanner
The Newberry Library

Indian villages are always composed of people from more than one tribe, even though they are generally identified with only one particular tribe. This mixture of tribal people in Indian communities was characteristic of the region around the base of Lake Michigan, including the Chicago area, as well as other parts of the country.

There were many reasons for people from several tribes to be living in an Indian village as minority populations. Some might be captives brought back from warfare in another region and incorporated in the tribe. Indian people have always been great travelers and traders, and occasionally married young women they met in the villages of trading partners. When Native American peoples visited allied tribes, they might stay a year or two before returning home, sometimes bringing back friends for a return visit. Indian people have always been known for their hospitality, and were proud to be able to entertain travelers as well as official couriers and delegations arriving on inter-tribal business.

Disagreements and sporadic warfare led to the appearance of small groups from other tribes in any major Indian settlement. Since each village or band tried to achieve a consensus in decision-making, the minority faction might voluntarily move to another town to end the dissension. Warfare also brought about the migration of entire communities,which moved into the territory of another tribe with permission to reside as guests of the host tribe. In major warfare along the American frontier, warriors and their families from eight or ten allied tribes periodically formed a multi-tribal military center that continued in existence for several years. When the tribal groups in the military center dispersed, they often took with them comrades in arms from another tribe.

Epidemic disease was another factor causing new population mixtures in Indian villages. Survivors of an epidemic usually abandoned the site of contamination and went to live with other people. Often their numbers were too small and they were too weak to continue alone. Religious fervor also produced new combinations of tribal people, as converts flocked to the home village of a new prophet or messianic leader.

Non-Indian people also lived in Indian villages of the Chicago district, as they did in other parts of North America. The fur traders who travelled regularly from Montreal or Three Rivers in Canada, and later from St. Louis, Albany, Mackinac Island, Philadelphia, or Pittsburgh lived part of the year in Indian towns. Often the traders had Indian families. These traders were of diverse European and African origin, adding to the complexity of populations in the Indian communities. In the seventeenth and eighteenth centuries, genetic heritage was not a matter of critical importance. If non-Indians lived according to Indian customs, they were accepted as relatives and kinfolk, though the assignment of clan affiliation presented a problem. White captives who were children were raised as though they were of Indian origin.

All of these factors affected the population composition of the Indian villages of the Chicago area and surrounding country at one time or another during the past three hundred years. Although historical records for events creating population mixtures exist only for a little over three centuries in the upper Great Lakes, oral traditions provide knowledge of similar occurrences for a much longer period of time.

The group of Indian villages located in the present state of Illinois and on the west bank of the Mississippi river, with large communities on the Illinois river, were known to the first French explorers as the Illinois Indians. These people were involved in the capture and trading of captives from tribes living to the southwest of their own homelands. In French records, these captives were called "panis," apparently an interpretation of "Pawnee," though the term referred to Indian slaves from any tribe west of the Mississippi river. So early Illinois Indian villages could include western Indian slaves. These "panis" were also reported in census records of the mid-eighteenth century for French and Indian communities on the Straits of Mackinac, Detroit, and Fort Miami (present Fort Wayne, Indiana).

The vicinity of modern Chicago has never been a favored site for Indian habitation. The sand dunes and swamps, with restricted timber and agricultural land, did not attract large numbers of Indian people. In the late seventeenth century, when there was a fortified post at Chicago for a brief time, Miami Indian people were living south of present Chicago near the bend of the Calumet river and on the Fox river about forty miles west of Chicago. These Miami, whose language is the same as the Illinois, may have been in the process of returning to their customary home base on the Wabash river of Indiana after fleeing temporarily from the route of Iroquois war parties from New York. The Miami village near the Calumet River nevertheless was attacked in 1687.

In the 1680s, the principal concentration of Indian people in northern Illinois was the vicinity of Fort St. Louis, established by Rene Robert Cavelier, Sieur de La Salle, in 1682 at Starved Rock, an island in the Illinois river near present Utica, Illinois about ninety miles southwest of Chicago. In addition to the large Kaskaskia village, Shawnee and Miami settled near the fort, which was the objective of an Iroquois expedition in 1683. The long period of Iroquois warfare involving Indians living far north and south of the Great Lakes came to an end with a peace treaty signed in Montreal in 1701. The Kaskaskia representatives from Illinois probably travelled the longest distance to take part in the councils.

Although the Potawatomi became the principal residents of the Chicago area during the eighteenth century, other Great Lakes Indians continued to make their homes for at least part of the year along the branches of the Chicago river and the portage to the Des Plaines river, a well-used route from Lake Michigan to the Illinois river, continuing to the Mississippi river and the Gulf of Mexico. It became a site for prosperous trading posts. Another period of warfare between the French and their Indian allies on one hand and the Mesquakie [Fox] and their allies as opponents, brought a group of Sauk and Mesquakie to the Chicago area in 1742-1743, but they soon moved westward to the Mississippi River Valley, further from French authority.

By the mid-eighteenth century, Potawatomi began expanding around the lower end of Lake Michigan from their headquarters towns on the St. Joseph river of southwestern Michigan. The Calumet river system offered particularly attractive sites for villages, but others moved along the western shore of Lake Michigan through northwestern Indiana to present day Chicago, Milwaukee and the Door Peninsula of Wisconsin. Imperial warfare between France and England, ending with the Treaty of Paris in 1763, was a factor in bringing Ottawa and Ojibwa [or Chippewa] Indians into northern Illinois and the Chicago vicinity in the 1760s. In 1760 the French established a fort at present Ottawa, Illinois a short distance above the site of La Salle's Fort St. Louis, a stretch of the river traditionally occupied by Illinois Indian villages. Apparently, pro-French Ottawa Indians from near Detroit moved to Fort Ottawa when the British took over the French fort at Detroit in 1760.

The resistance movement to prevent the British from occupying French forts in the Great Lakes Region, a movement headed by Pontiac, the Ottawa leader from Detroit, continued in the Illinois country until 1769. Indian people denied the right of European powers to turn over the French forts in Indian country to the British. Although Pontiac was unsuccessful in his attempted siege of Detroit in 1763, his followers relocated on the Maumee river of Ohio, west of present Toledo. Pontiac himself and some of his strongest supporters came to Illinois to prevent the British from occupying Fort Chartres. The

Illinois Indians, then concentrated in the southwestern part of the state near Kaskaskia and Cahokia, urged him to continue the ultimately unsuccessful struggle. He had other adherents among the Ojibwa of the present Upper Peninsula of Michigan near Sault Ste. Marie, Ottawa from the northwestern Lower Peninsula of Michigan near present Petoskey, a few Sauk from northern Illinois, and some Potawatomi. Warriors from these tribal groups congregated at Chicago in the late 1760s, to enter battle if Pontiac decided on further militant action.

Despite the fact that a number of Ottawa and Ojibwa continued to live in the Potawatomi communities around Chicago and present Milwaukee, and even further north on the Lake Michigan shoreline, the local leadership was clearly in the hands of the Potawatomi by the 1770s. Nevertheless, in dealing with Indian people of the southern end of Lake Michigan, the American government usually called them the "United Bands of Chippewa, Ottawa and Potawatomi." These were the Indian people whom settlers met when they came to Chicago in the 1830s.

By the time of the Treaty of Chicago in 1833, whereby the Potawatomi gave up the last of their lands and reservations, the closest towns to metropolitan Chicago were at the bend of the Calumet river, south of Chicago, and on the Des Plaines river north of the portage from the south branch of the Chicago river. Both the portage site and the mouth of the Chicago river were important trading sites. Important traders at Chicago after the 1770s were of Haitian, French, Scots, and English origin. By the 1830s, too, the population composition of the Potawatomi towns further from Chicago included other minorities. Potawatomi who moved as far west as the Rock River met the Winnebago, and villages included people from both tribal groups. Other Potawatomi became followers of the Kickapoo prophet, Kennekuk, and lived with his band on Sugar Creek close to the present Indiana state line about one hundred twenty miles south of Chicago. Potawatomi living on the upper Illinois river had Kickapoo living amongst them.

The above discussion indicates tribal mixtures in Chicago and surrounding territory for the period prior to the removal of the Potawatomi after 1837. There are different reasons for the numerous tribal people in present day Chicago. Some came from distant reservations for work opportunities. The largest influx came as a consequence of the federal government relocation program following World War II. Yet many Potawatomi who were removed later returned to the rural areas of southeastern Wisconsin, northern Illinois, and northwestern Indiana.

Map of Indian Villages in Illinois, 1830

Helen Tanner

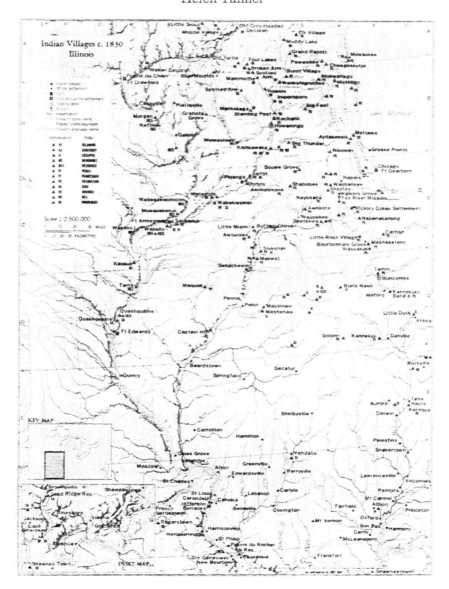

Notable American Indian Men and Women of the Greater Chicago and Illinois Region: Historic Period, 1673-1878

Virgil Vogel

Illinois:

Chicagou

Ducoigne

Baptiste Peoria

Shawnee:

Tecumseh

Sauk:

Black Hawk

Kickapoo:

Kenekuk

Potawatomi & Ottawa:

Black Partridge

Billy Caldwell

Half Day

Menominee

Monee

Archange Ouilmette

Alexander Robinson

Shabbona

Waubansee

Watseka

Chicagou
Illinois - Michigamea
16--? - 1754

Chicagou (Chikagou, Checagou, etc.) was a village chief of the Michigamea tribe of the Illinois confederacy. In the early eighteenth century they lived in the vicinity of Ft. Chartres on the Mississippi, near Prairie du Rocher. Our knowledge of him is scanty, and is found chiefly in a few references in the *Jesuit Relations* and in the official account of his visit to France in 1725.

It was in that year that Chicagou was chosen, along with a delegation of the Oto, Osage, and Missouri tribes, to go to Paris to meet the boy king, Louis XV, along with other members of the court and agents of the India Company. The trip was arranged by Etienne V. de Bourgmont of the India Company and the Jesuit priest Nicholas Ignace Beaubois. The object of the venture was to impress the Indians with the grandeur and power of the French king and nation.

The party arrived in France September 20, 1725, and its members were lavishly entertained and showered with gifts. Besides meeting the young king, they also met the Duke and Duchess of Orleans, the Duke of Bourbon, and officials of the India Company. A detailed account of their visit was published in the *Mercur de France* (December 1725) and the *London Postman* (January 27, 1726). At each meeting of the Indians with the French, elaborate orations were exchanged, translated by Bourgmont and Brisbois. It is reported that Chicagou drew the most attention "because he was in Savage attire or because he was a Christian and was introduced by a missionary."

According to the published report of his address to the king, Chicagou said:

> I no longer regret having suffered so much and having left my wife and children and all my Nation, because today I see the Father of all the French in the midst of his chiefs. I myself am a Chief and am well thought of in my Nation, but I now see that I am nothing in comparison to you, to whom so many Chiefs and as many people as there are trees in our forests give their obedience.

Chicagou also said "we are French at heart" and would obey the king. He described the Foxes as the common enemy. The Duchess of Orleans presented Chicagou with a gold embossed and bejeweled snuffbox, which he treasured for many years.

Upon his return to America, Chicagou told his people of the wondrous things he had seen. He spoke of five cabins, one on top of the other, as high as the tallest trees. There were as many people on the streets of Paris as blades of grass on the prairies or mosquitoes in the woods. The French rode about in moving cabins, and made long journeys in them. The had long cabins for the care of the sick and injured, where their surgeons performed wonderful cures. His people found it hard to believe these reports, some saying he had been bribed or fascinated by some charm which affected his eyes.

Chicagou showed his loyalty to the French by rallying Indians to their aid after some two hundred French settlers were massacred by the Natchez in present Mississippi on October 28, 1729, and others were attacked by the Yazoo. Leading a delegation of Michigamea, Chicagou joined with the Kaskaskia under Mamantouensa, declaring to Louisiana Governor Perrier at New Orleans:

> We have come from a great distance to weep with you for the deaths of the French, and to offer our Warriors to strike those Nations whom you may wish to designate. You have but to speak. When I went over to France, the king promised his protection for the Prayer [Christian Faith], and recommended me never to abandon it. I will always remember it. Grant them your protection to us and to our black Robes.

Indians from the Ft. Chartres area joined with the Kickapoo and Mascouten in assisting the French siege of the Foxes, August 17 to September 9, 1730, which resulted in near annihilation of the Foxes. That expedition was led by the commandant from Ft. Chartres, St. Ange, but the location of the incident is in dispute. It is not known whether Chicagou participated.

In 1736 Chicagou showed his fealty to the French by joining an expedition against the Chickasaw under the command of Diron d'Artaguiette, inspector-general of Louisiana. The Chickasaw, of northern Mississippi, were allies of the British and had been attacking French settlements. The French-led punitive expedition, leaving Ft. Chartres, included contingents of Indians from several tribes. An additional force under Governor Bienville failed to arrive in time. D'Artaguiette was attacked by the Chickasaw on March 25, 1736, his forces were decimated, and the commander himself was captured and burned. Chicagou survived and returned to Illinois.

Records of Ft. Chartres indicate that "Chigagoua chief of the village of the Metchigamias" sold a parcel of land to one Michel Vien on July 8, 1746. A notary document dated December 15, 1756, involving this parcel refers to the "defunct Chicagou, Chief of the village of the Metchigamia." It is believed that he died in 1754.

In assessing Chicagou's role it seems that the excessive loyalty to the French on the part of Chicagou and the other Illinois involved them in nearly continuous warfare and contributed to the precipitate decline of their population.

Some writers have thought that the city of Chicago was named for Chicagou. This is not possible, because the site of the city was called Chicagou by La Salle as early as September 1, 1683, when the Indian Chicagou was probably not yet born. Moreover, tribes did not name places for individuals, and Chicagou's tribe, the Michigamea, never lived near Chicago. Finally, we have the written testimony of Henri Joutel, in 1687, that the place called "Chicagou" received the name "from the quantity of garlic which grows in this district, in the woods."

Sources

Clarence W. Alvord, *The Illinois Country 1673-1818* (Chicago: Loyola University Press, 1965), 170-171, 177-178, 223.

Margaret Kimball Brown and Lawrie Cena Dean, *The Village of Chartres in Colonial Illinois 1720-1765* (New Orleans: Polyanthos, 1977).

Richard N. Ellis and Charles R. Stern, "An Indian Delegation in France, 1725," *Journal Illinois State Historical Society*, Vol. 67, No. 4 (September, 1974), pp. 385-405.

Raymond E. Hauser, "The Illinois Indian Tribe: From Autonomy and Self-Sufficiency to Dependency and Depopulation," *Journal Illinois State Historical Society*, Vol. 69, No. 2 (May, 1976), pp. 127-138.

Edna Kenton, ed., *Black Gown and Redskins* (London: Longmans Green Co., 1954), pp. 426-428.

Joseph L. Peyser, "The 1730 Fox Fort . . . ," *Journal Illinois State Historical Society*, Vol. 73, No. 3 (Autumn, 1980), pp. 201-213.

James Scott, *The Illinois Nation*, Part 1 (Streator: The Streator Historical Society, 1973), pp. 27-28.

Joseph J. Thompson, "Chicagou—the Grand Chief of the Illinois, Protonym of the Western Metropolis," *Illinois Catholic Historical Review*, Vol. 7 (1924-25), pp. 332-337.

Reuben Gold Thwaites, *Jesuit Relations and Allied Documents*, 73 Vols. (Cleveland: The Burrows Bros. Co., 1896-1901), Vol. 68, doc. cciii.

Jean Baptiste Ducoigne
Illinois-Kaskaskia
1755-1832

Jean Baptiste Ducoigne (De Coigne, De Couagne, Du Quoin, etc.) was the son of an Indian woman named Elizabeth Michel Rouensa and a Frenchman whose name was written as "De Couagne" in the baptismal record of their son Louis, born January 20, 1750, according to the register of the parish of St. Anne of Ft. Chartres, signed by Father J. Gagnon. (Charles de Couagne, baptized in 1651, was a Montreal merchant who married three times and fathered fourteen children. [Pease & Werner, *French Foundations*, p. 169n.] The De Couagne family is mentioned in Thwaites, *Jesuit Relations*, Vol. 69, p. 253.)

The date of the birth of Jean Baptiste Ducoigne has not been established, although Stanley Faye placed it in 1755. Louis Ducoigne was apparently only seventeen years old when he became chief of the Kaskaskia in 1767. On July 3, 1767, Edward Cole, of Ft. Chartres, wrote to George Croghan:

> The nation assembled before me in order to have another chief-—young Dequoney being the next heir, he was unanimously pitched on if agreeable to me. I could have no objection knowing him to be a fine young fellow not Debauched with Liquors, and from the readiness he shows to receive advice and his Good behaviour [sic], makes me think he will become one of the Greatest chiefs in this country. (Clarence W. Alvord, *The New Regime, 1765-67* [Springfield: Collections Illinois State Historical Library, Vol. 9: 1916], p. 581.)

By the time of George Rogers Clark's capture of Illinois from the British in 1778, the Kaskaskia chief was Jean Baptiste Ducoigne, apparently a younger brother of Louis. Stanley Faye says that Jean Baptiste was about ten years old in 1765, or five years younger than Louis. (Stanley Faye, "Illinois Indians on the Lower Mississippi, 1771-1782," *Journal Illinois State Historical Society*, Vol. 39 [March, 1942], pp. 57-72.) Faye adds that Jean Baptiste became chief in 1774 at age 19. At that time he went with about 300 of his people to Arkansas River, where he asked the Spanish for land on White River, but was refused. Later, however, it was granted as a reward for pillaging the English. The Kaskaskia returned to Illinois in 1777.

When, on July 4 of the next year, George Rogers Clark with one hundred fifty men made his bloodless conquest of the Illinois settlements, he received the support of Ducoigne, who went on a mission to the erstwhile enemies of the Illinois, the Chickasaw, to secure their adherence to the American cause. At first he failed, but succeeded on another mission in 1782. Meanwhile, he supplied Clark's men with venison. His tribe was host to representatives of other midwest tribes called to council by Clark. In 1781 Ducoigne visited Ft. Pitt and Richmond, bringing back dispatches for Clark at Louisville. On September 25, 1781, Clark gave $900 in depreciated Virginia currency to an Ohio River merchant in part payment "for a Rifle Gun for John Baptist the Indian Chief." (Alvord, *Kaskaskia Records*, pp. 248-249; George Rogers Clark, *George Rogers Clark Papers*, ed. James Alton James [Springfield: Collections Illinois State Historical Library, Vol. 8, 1912], pp. 261, 418, 555.)

In the late 1780s, when the Ohio tribes were preparing to defend their territory from American occupation, Ducoigne and the Illinois tribes were in danger from hostile Kickapoo, Piankashaw, and Shawnee because of their close ties to the Americans. In the winter of 1787-1788 the Kickapoo attacked the Illinois, killing five men and six children besides capturing eight persons. The following year the American residents about Kaskaskia showed great concern for the safety of Chief Jean Baptiste Ducoigne and his people. His life was threatened by Piankashaw, Delaware, Shawnee and Fox Indians from west of the Mississippi. It was supposed that their hostility was engendered by the Spanish and by Americans who had migrated to their territory.

Maj. John Hamtramck at Vincennes received reports from Kaskaskia on October 29, 1789, by John R. Jones and John Edgar, of Indian provocations and of danger to Ducoigne. Ducoigne was reported by Jones to have found a fresh trail made by "a large party of Kickapoo for war, making towards the Ohio." Jones further wrote:

> For near three weeks we have kept a constant guard both night and day for fear of the menaces of the Indians, enticed by the white men [Spanish], being put into execution. Indeed we know not when there is danger, as almost every person that comes from Miserie [St. Genevieve] and St. Louis bring us accounts & letters, that we are to be massacred in the village, sometimes by the Delawares and Shawanese, with the Piankeshaws, and at other times by the Sacs and Renards [Foxes], who in seeking for Ducoigne, will kill the Americans as his friends; though for my part, I believe that most of these stories are fabricated on the other side on purpose to frighten us away. (Alvord, *Kaskaskia Records*, p. 516.)

Edgar at the same time added his apprehensive report:

> These Indians [Piankashaw] have hatred enough to the Americans without being pushed on by white men; for this reason I am fearful of Ducoigne's life this winter, as the Piankeshaws threaten hard because he is a friend to Americans.

Anthony Wayne's victory over the Indians in Ohio at Fallen Timbers in 1794 seems to have alleviated the supposed danger from some tribes. However, in ensuing years, the Illinois were harassed by their old enemies, the Chickasaw, and in 1797 the Kickapoo made the last recorded attack on the Illinois during that century, causing Ducoigne to send this message to the commandant at Kaskaskia:

> I understand that the Kickapoos has proposed war with America, which I am very well satisfied in it, for they have killed my friend . . . which satisfied me, they are determined for war . . . I expect to be with you in the space of Six weeks, & then I will inform you better things.

In 1803, the transfer of Louisiana back to the French and its prompt purchase by the United States ended American expectations of attack from the West. In that same year, on August 7, at Vincennes, Ducoigne, with representatives of several other tribes, signed a treaty with Governor Harrison giving the United States three tracts of one square mile each on the road from Vincennes to Clarksville for "houses of entertainment for accommodation of travellers."

Only six days later, a second treaty, with the Kaskaskia alone, gave up all Indian land except 350 acres near Kaskaskia, reserved by act of Congress, and 1,280 acres elsewhere. In return the government was to give the Indians an annuity of $1,000 and build a house for the chief, Jean B. Ducoigne, and fence for him 100 acres. In addition, the government was to pay $100 a year for seven years for a Catholic priest for the Indians, $300 for erecting a church, and $580 in debt payments. These rather petty benefits were to be considered full compensation for their relinquishment of all lands named. The treaty was signed by Ducoigne and his son Louis, along with four other Indians.

By 1807 the Illinois were reduced to about 500 individuals, when the Kickapoo attacked again, killing a man and capturing thirty horses. Ducoigne asked for federal protection as promised to the Kaskaskia in the treaty of August 13, 1803.

By the time the second war with Great Britain began in 1812, the Illinois Indians were too few in number, and too acculturated, to be a threat to anyone. As in the American Revolution, they supported the American cause, and in so doing earned the enmity of the majority of midwest Indians who were pro-British. Governor Ninian Edwards considered it inadvisable for the Illinois Indians to go hunting, because they might be attacked by hostile Indians or by whites unable to distinguish one from the other. Therefore, they had to be provided with subsistence by the territorial government. Despite their loyalty, the pliable Illinois were soon to lose their last foothold in Illinois.

On September 25, 1818, another treaty was signed at Edwardsville, in which the Peoria, who were not included in the earlier treaty, assented to its provisions. The treaty awarded $2,000 in merchandise to the signatory tribes, plus an annuity of $300 to the Peoria for twelve years. The government also reserved to the Peoria 640 acres in Missouri, to include their village on Blackwater River. This treaty was signed by twenty-five Indians, including eleven Peoria, four Kaskaskia (among which was Louis Jefferson "Ducouagne") three Michigamia, five Cahokia, and two Tamaroa.

The final end to the presence of the Illinois in the state named for them came as a result of the treaty they signed with William Clark at Castor Hill, Missouri, October 27, 1832. Jean Baptiste Ducoigne was not a signer, for he died shortly before that time, at an unknown date. In this document, the five fragmented bands which "formerly composed the Illinois nation of Indians" ceded all lands reserved to them by the treaty of Vincennes of August 13, 1803, "reserving however to Ellen Decoigne the daughter of their late chief who has married a white man, the tract of land of about three hundred and fifty acres near the town of Kaskaskia, which was secured to said tribe by the Act of Congress of 3d March, 1793."

The Kaskaskia relinquished their $1,000 annuity and their salt annuity under the treaty of Ft. Wayne of June 7, 1803. All remaining land in Illinois and Missouri still claimed by the Indians was ceded. In return the United States gave the combined tribes one hundred fifty sections of land on the Osage River in present Kansas forever, or as long as they lived on it as a tribe. They would receive an annuity of $3,000 for ten years. Because the Indians had not understood the treaty of Edwardsville, which ceded their claims in Missouri, the United States compensated them with various provisions and promised one year's sustenance in their new home.

The hapless Illinois were soon to learn that "forever" was a short time so far as the government was concerned. In 1867 they were removed to northeastern Oklahoma, in consequence of a new treaty. There, at present, perhaps 150 mixed-blood descendants live near the village of Peoria, and still maintain a tribal organization under the name of Peoria.

In the view of early Illinois governor John Reynolds, Ducoigne "was a cunning man, and had considerable talents . . . well qualified to take charge of his nation in their present condition." According to him, it was Ducoigne's assertion that neither he nor his people had ever shed the blood of a white person. As for cunning, it seems in retrospect that the greater degree of cunning was exercised by the government treaty makers. General (later President) William Henry Harrison, who negotiated several treaties leading to Indian dispossession and removal, spoke of Ducoigne as "a gentlemanly man, by no means addicted to drink, possessing a very strong inclination to live like a white man; indeed has done so as far as his means will allow." In a letter to the secretary of war, Harrison added, "Ducoigne's long and well proved friendship for the United States has gained him the hatred of all the other chiefs and ought to be an inducement with us to provide as well for his happiness as his safety."

In 1844, only twelve years after the Illinois moved west, a new town was laid out in Perry County, Illinois, and named Du Quoin in honor of the late chief. It was never incorporated and in 1854 and subsequently most of its residents moved to a new town also called Du Quoin, which was laid out on the Illinois Central railroad in 1853. The small village at the former site has since been called Old Du Quoin. The chief's name, spelled as one word, Duquoin, was given to a village in Harper County, Kansas.

Sources

Clarence W. Alvord, ed. *Kaskaskia Records, 1778-1790* (Springfield: Trustees of the Illinois State Historical Library, 1909), pp. 248-249, 513-516.

_____, ed., *The New Regime, 1765-67* (Springfield: Collections Illinois State Historical Society, Vol. 9: 1916), p. 581.

Emily Blasingham, "The Depopulation of the Illinois Indians," *Ethnohistory*, Vol. 3, No. 3 (Summer 1956), pp. 193-224.

_____, *ibid.*, Part 2, Vol. 3, No. 4 (Fall 1956), pp. 361-412.

Margaret Brown and Lawrie C. Dean, eds., *The Village of Chartres in Colonial Illinois, 1720-1765* (New Orleans: Polyanthos, 1977), pp. 161-162, 603-605.

Stanley Faye, "Illinois Indians on the Lower Mississippi, 1771-1782," *Journal of Illinois State Historical Society*, Vol. 35 (March 1942), pp. 57-72.

Grant Foreman, "Illinois and Her Indians," *Papers in Illinois History* (Springfield: Illinois State Historical Society, 1940), pp. 67-111.

Raymond E. Hauser, "The Illinois Indian Tribe ... ," *Journal Illinois State Historical Society*, Vol. 69, No. 2 (May, 1976), pp. 127-138.

_____, "Warfare and the Illinois Indian Tribe During the Seventeenth Century," *The Old Northwest*, Vol. 10, No. 4 (Winter, 1984-85), pp. 367-388.

Louise Houghton, *Our Debt to the Red Man* (Boston: The Stratford Co., 1918), pp. 80-81.

James Alton James, ed., *George Rogers Clark Papers, 1771-1781* (Springfield: Collections Illinois State Historical Library, Volume 8, 1912), pp. 261, 418, 555.

Charles J. Kappler, ed., *Indian Treaties* (New York: Interland Publishing Co., 1972), pp. 61, 67-68, 165-166, 376-377, 662.

Theodore Pease and Raymond Werner: *The French Foundations, 1680-1693* (Springfield: Trustees of the Illinois State Historical Library, 1934), pp. 169n, 176.

John Reynolds, *Pioneer History of Illinois* (Ann Arbor: University Microfilms, 1968, reprint), p. 23.

James Scott, *The Illinois Nation*, Part 1 (Streator: The Streator Historical Society, 1973), pp. 36, 39-40.

Reuben G. Thwaites, ed., *Jesuit Relations*, Vol. 69 (Cleveland: The Burrows Company, 1896-1901), p. 253.

Cyrus Thomas, "Ducoigne, Jean Baptiste," in F. W. Hodge, Ed: *Handbook of the American Indian North of Mexico*, Vol. 1 (Bureau of Ethnology Bulletin 30, Washington, D.C.: Smithsonian Institution, 1907-1910), p. 405.

Virgil J. Vogel, *Indian Place Names in Illinois* (Springfield: Illinois State Historical Society, 1962), pp. 29-30.

Muriel H. Wright, *A Guide to the Indian Tribes of Oklahoma* (Norman: University of Oklahoma Press, 1965), p. 209.

Baptiste Peoria (Lanepeshaw)
Peoria-Illinois
ca. 1793-September 13, 1873

Baptiste Peoria was born in Illinois near the junction of the Kankakee and Des Plaines Rivers. His father, Baptiste, was a French-
Canadian trader among the Illinois; his mother was the daughter of a
Peoria sub-chief. Young Baptiste became a speaker of French, English, and several Indian languages. Although unschooled, the government used his services for thirty years as an interpreter in treaty
negotiations.

At the treaty of Edwardsville, September 25, 1818, Baptiste Peoria
signed for the Peoria tribe as "Battice, or Baptist, his *X* mark," signi-
fying his probable illiteracy. By this document the Peoria ceded their
Illinois lands, as the other Illinois tribes had already done, in return
for an annuity of $300 for twelve years and the grant of one section of
640 acres on the Blackwater River of Missouri.

In 1832, following the Castor Hill treaty, the Peoria joined with
their other Illinois brethren in moving to the Osage River in present
Miami County, Kansas. After the death of Ducoigne in 1832, Baptiste
Peoria eventually became the spokesman for the Illinois. Already on
November 12, 1833, Peoria aided government agent John Dougherty
and others in negotiating a treaty to end fighting between the Pawnee and several immigrant tribes in Kansas, including the Delaware.

In Kansas, Peoria operated a store at his home at Baptiste Springs,
the site of the present town of Paola. Some time after 1848 he married his third wife, the former Mary Ann Isaacs, a member of the New
York Brothertown (Mohican) Indians and widow of the noted Wea,
Christmas Dagney.

In 1850 the agent reported that the Peoria had taken the pledge to
abstain from drinking ardent spirits, a movement promoted by the
interpreter Baptiste Peoria, a former inebriate who was given much
of the credit for the progress made by the Indians. In 1852 the agent
reported that the Wea, Piankashaw and Peoria tribes would, in
sobriety, "compare favorably with the same amount of white population . . . from any part of the country."

In 1855 John Beach, the Sauk and Fox agent, located his agency at
Baptiste Springs, the home of interpreter Baptiste Peoria. Beach
wrote:

> The character of this man for honesty, truth, and the great influ-
> ence he wields over the Indians, together with his expanded
> knowledge of their affairs, seemed to make it necessary that I

have him near me. Much of the credit for sobriety and industry, and the consequent advancement in civilization, which the Indians seem entitled to, is due to Battiest Peoria.

On May 30, 1854, the Kaskaskia, Peoria, and other Illinois tribes united with the Piankashaw and Wea, becoming known as the Consolidated Peoria. On that date these tribes ceded to the United States all the Kansas lands they had been granted in the Castor Hill treaty of 1832, receiving in return 160 acres for every individual in addition to ten sections reserved for the tribe. The "permanent" annuities of $3,800 due from previous treaties were relinquished, in return for $66,000 to be paid in six annual installments.

In the schedule attached to the treaty the Baptiste Peoria family was shown as consisting of eight persons, three males and five females, who received a total of 1,280 acres. In addition, the family of Joe Peoria, apparently a son, received 640 acres for four persons. Interestingly, the signatory list attached to this treaty names Baptiste Peoria as a United States interpreter, not as an Indian signer.

In the city of Washington, on February 23, 1867, the consolidated Peoria and several other tribes signed the so-called "omnibus" treaty. By its terms, the last of the Illinois were deprived of the residue of the lands reserved to them "forever" by the treaty of Castor Hill in 1832. Their Kansas lands were to be sold and the proceeds used to purchase new lands for them from the Quapaw, Seneca, and Shawnee in northeastern Oklahoma. Individual Indians of the Peoria, Kaskaskia, Wea and Piankashaw tribes could stay in Kansas if they would give up all tribal rights and become American citizens. Fifty-five did so. The government was to seek the return to the Indians of taxes illegally collected from them by the State of Kansas. The Indians were to leave the state within two years. This treaty, the last with the Peoria, was signed with an x by Baptist Peoria, in behalf of his tribe.

The aging chief moved with his people to their final home, where, according to Clark Foreman, "they received much help and encouragement in opening up their little farms from Baptiste Peoria, their intelligent and progressive chief, and a leading man in the confederacy."

In the new reserve, in present Ottawa County, Oklahoma, Baptiste Peoria died on September 13, 1873. He was buried in the Peoria cemetery, which is still maintained a few miles west of the village of Peoria, Oklahoma. That place, like several other Peorias, is named for the tribe. However, the town of Paola, county seat of Miami County, Kansas, is named for him. Its peculiar spelling represents the pronunciation of his name by those Indians, such as the Miami, who were unused to pronouncing the sound of "r."

Sources

Hiram Beckwith, *The Illinois and Indiana Indians* (New York: Arno Press, 1975, reprint), pp. 115-116.

Clark Foreman, *Last Trek of the Indians* (Chicago: University of Chicago Press, 1946), pp. 151, 182, 202-205.

Louise Houghton, *Our Debt to the Red Man* (Boston: The Stratford Co., 1918), pp. 74-75.

Charles J. Kappler, ed., *Indian Treaties, 1778-1883* (New York: Interland Publishing Co., 1972), pp. 165-166, 636-641, 967.

John Rydjord, *Kansas Place Names* (Norman: University of Oklahoma Press, 1972), pp. 17, 429.

James Scott, *The Illinois Nation*, 2 Vols. (Streator: Streator Historical Society, 1973), Vol. 2, pp. 50-51.

Muriel Wright, *A Guide to the Indian Tribes of Oklahoma* (Norman: University of Oklahoma Press, 1965), pp. 207-209.

Tecumseh
Shawnee
1768-1813

No list of outstanding Indians is complete without the name of Tecumseh, who has been called "the most extraordinary Indian character in United States history." He was born in the Shawnee village of Piqua, Ohio, in 1768, the son of a chief. His father and two brothers were killed in border wars with whites. He became an advocate of Indian unity and travelled widely to build a common policy in dealing with the white man. He held that the land was the common property of all Indians, and none might sell it without the consent of all. Not aggressive as he has been portrayed, his aim was peaceful resistance to further erosion of the land base, through inter-tribal unity. He joined with his brother, Tenskwatawa, "the Prophet," in urging a return to Indian ways. They opposed the use of liquor, forbade torture, and encouraged agriculture and monogamy. An inter-tribal village established by them at the junction of the Tippecanoe and Wabash Rivers in Indiana was destroyed, during Tecumseh's absence, by troops led by General William Henry Harrison (later the ninth president), on November 7, 1811. It was an act which ensured Indian support of the British in the War of 1812. Tecumseh enlisted in the British cause, was reportedly given the rank and uniform of a brigadier general, and was killed in battle near Chatham, Ontario, October 5, 1813.

His name has been spelled and translated in various ways. Jacob Piatt Dunn called him Tecumtha, "going across or going over." Perhaps no Indian except Osceola has had more places named for him. Tecumseh, Michigan, was named for him only eleven years after his death. Eleven towns and topographic features in the United States bear his name, while he is honored by three more places in Canada.

Sources

David C. Cooke, *Tecumseh, Destiny's Warrior* (New York: Julian Messner, 1959), juvenile.

R. David Edmunds, *Tecumseh and the Quest for Indian Leadership* (Boston: Little Brown Co., 1984).

Carl F. Klinck, *Tecumseh, Fact and Fiction in Early Records* (Englewood

Cliffs, N.J.: Prentice-Hall, 1961), primary source materials.

James Mooney, "Tecumseh," in F. W. Hodge, Ed: *Handbook of the American Indian North of Mexico*, Vol. 2 (Bureau of Ethnology Bulletin 30, Washington, D.C.: Smithsonian Institution, 1907-1910), p. 714.

Glenn Tucker, *Tecumseh, Vision of Glory* (Indianapolis: Bobbs Merrill, 1956).

Black Hawk, Makataimeshekiakiak
(Black Sparrow Hawk)
Sauk
1767-1838

Black Hawk, by his own account a Sauk war chief like his father Pyesa, was born at Saukenuk, at the mouth of Rock River, Illinois. While a young man he distinguished himself in war with the Osage and Cherokee, and during the War of 1812, he fought for the British. However, he is known to history for his courageous leadership of the only serious struggle by an Illinois Indian tribe to save or recover its homeland from white occupation. The Black Hawk War, which lasted from April to August, 1832, is described in Chapter 1 above. It began after the Sauk and allied Foxes had been forced in 1830-31 to move across the Mississippi into Iowa in consequence of a fraudulent treaty signed with General Harrison by Quashquame in 1804.

The Indians were forced to leave before harvesting their corn crop. After a hungry winter in Iowa, Black Hawk recrossed the Mississippi on April 5, 1832, with nine hundred followers, including men, women, and children. They were pursued first by Illinois militia, whom they defeated at Stillman's Run on May 14, and later by federal troops and Wisconsin volunteers. After numerous skirmishes, the Sauk, who failed to win support from other tribes, fled across southwestern Wisconsin, reaching the Mississippi below the mouth of the Bad Axe, where on August 1 they were nearly annihilated by their pursuers. Black Hawk and a few others escaped but surrendered a few weeks later at Prairie du Chien.

With a few companions, including one of his sons, he was taken by boat to Jefferson Barracks, Missouri, where he was held in chains through the winter, then taken to Washington to meet his nemesis, President Andrew Jackson. According to Black Hawk:

> He said he wished to know the cause of my going to war against his white children. I thought he ought to have known this before; and, consequently, said but little to him about it as I expected he knew as well as I could tell him.

He was confined for a month at Fortress Monroe, Virginia, along with his son Nasheaskuk, and the Winnebago, White Cloud. There, Black Hawk and his companions sat for portraits by Robert M. Sully, Samuel M. Brooks, John Wesley Jarvis, Charles Bird King, and J. O. Lewis. Earlier, at Jefferson Barracks, Black Hawk's portrait was painted by George Catlin.

Next, Black Hawk was taken on a tour of eastern cities, designed to impress him with white power. To white audiences who seldom saw an Indian, he and his son were lionized as heroes. Returning to Iowa under the guardianship of his rival, Keokuk, Black Hawk settled in a wickiup beside the Iowa River, together with his only wife, a daughter, and two sons. There, he dictated his autobiography to the educated French-Potawatomi, Antoine Le Claire. It was published in 1833, and again in several editions, the latest in 1955. In 1837 he made another trip to the east, during which Charles Bird King painted him for the last time. In 1838 Black Hawk moved his home to the banks of the Des Moines River in Van Buren County, and died there on October 3.

Black Hawk signed only one treaty with the United States, at St. Louis on May 13, 1816, where his name is written as "Mucketamachekaka, or Black Sparrow Hawk." The treaty ended hostilities of the War of 1812. It contained no new land cessions, but did contain a paragraph, unbeknown to Black Hawk, which confirmed the Quashquame treaty of 1804.

In Illinois the name of Black Hawk is commemorated in numerous places: on an island in Rock River at Rockford, city parks in Chicago and Rockford, a state park in Rock Island, and a forest preserve in Cook county. In addition, his name is on a township in Rock Island county, and several schools are named for him. State route #2 along Rock River is called the Black Hawk Trail. On a bluff above Rock River in Lowden State Park near Oregon, Illinois, stands a thirty-foot statue bearing his name, although its features are not his. When erected in 1911, it was intended by the sculptor, Lorado Taft, as a memorial to all Indians. A more representative, if less imposing, statue of Black Hawk stands before the Hauberg Museum in Black Hawk State Park, Rock Island. There are numerous places named for Black Hawk in Wisconsin and Iowa.

Sources

Black Hawk, *Black Hawk, an Autobiography*, ed. Donald Jackson (Urbana: University of Illinois Press, 1955).

Cecil Eby, *"That Disgraceful Affair,"* The Black Hawk War (New York: W. W. Norton, 1973).

William T. Hagan, *The Sac and Fox Indians* (Norman: University of Oklahoma Press, 1958).

John H. Hauberg, "The Black Hawk War, 1831-32," *Illinois State Historical Society, Transactions for the Year 1932* (Springfield: 1932), pp. 91-134.

James D. Horan, *The McKenney-Hall Portrait Gallery of American Indians* (New York: Crown Publishers, 1972), p. 168.

Charles J. Kappler, ed., *Indian Treaties* (New York: Interland Publishing Co., 1972), p. 128.

William F. Stark, *Along the Black Hawk Trail* (Sheboygan, Wis.: Zimmerman Press, 1984).

Frank E. Stevens, *The Black Hawk War* (Chicago: Frank E. Stevens, 1903).

John Swanton, "Black Hawk," in F. W. Hodge, ed., *Handbook of the American Indian North of Mexico*, Vol. 2, (Bureau of Ethnology Bulletin 30, Washington, D.C.: Smithsonian Institution, 1907-1910) pp. 150-152.

Virgil J. Vogel, *Indian Place Names in Illinois* (Springfield: Illinois Historical Society, 1962), pp. 160-162.

_____, *Iowa Place Names of Indian Origin* (Iowa City: University of Iowa Press, 1983), pp. 7-81.

Ellen M. Whitney, ed., *The Black Hawk War 1831-32* (Springfield: Collections Illinois State Historical Society, Vols. 35-38, 1970-78).

Kenekuk
Kickapoo
ca. 1785-1852

In the neighborhood of Danville, Illinois, in October 1832, a party of Kickapoo Indians encamped near the farm of Thomas Forsyth, a retired Indian agent. He visited them and recorded these impressions:

> I found them to be the Prophet or Preachers party . . . in every camp or lodge . . . a piece of flat wood hung up . . . on which were burned with a hot iron (apparently) a number of straight and crooked marks, this stick or board so marked they called their Bible. Those Indians told me that they worked six days and the seventh done [sic] no kind of work, but prayed to the Great Spirit, that no men of their community were allowed to have more than one wife, that none . . . were allowed to paint themselves, that they never made, or intended to make, war, against any people[;] that they never stole, tell lies or do anything bad . . . I should not be surprised, if this teaching of the Prophet of the Kickapoo Indians, is the commencement of religion ... it ought to be encouraged by the government as it inculcates peace and good will to all men.

The Kickapoo prophet's name was Kanakuk, Kenekuk, or Keannekuk (it is spelled several other ways). In a treaty signed at Fort Harrison, Indiana, June 4, 1816, his name is given as Kaanehkaka, or Drunkard's Son. The treaty of Castor Hill, Missouri, October 24, 1832, has his name as Ka-ana-kuck, the prophet. Dockstader interpreted his name as "putting his foot down," while Albert Gatschet held its meaning to be "foremost man."

Kenekuk did not join other Kickapoo leaders in a treaty ceding Illinois lands in 1819, and quite reasonably resisted, by delays and subterfuges, Superintendent William Clark's efforts to remove his band from Illinois. With about three hundred followers, some of them Potawatomi, he continued to live along the Vermilion or the Wabash until, in a treaty signed at Castor Hill, Missouri, on October 24, 1832, he finally yielded, and moved to Kansas with his people the next year. The movements of the various bands of Kickapoo before and after that date have been traced by A. M. Gibson, in *The Kickapoos* (1963), and by others.

Kenekuk continued to preach his religion until he died of smallpox in 1852. In different accounts his age has been given as 55 and 67. He was succeeded by his son John Kenekuk (as it is spelled in treaties of 1854 and 1862). The name of the elder Kenekuk is preserved in a village of that name in Atchison County, Kansas, not far from the Kickapoo reservation.

Sources

John Forsyth, memo in Emma Blair, translator, editor, annotated, and with bibliography and index by: *The Indian Tribes of the Upper Mississippi Valley and Region of the Great Lakes as described by Nicolas Perrot, French commandant in the Northwest; Bacqueville de la Potherie, French royal commissioner to Canada; Morrell Marston, American army officer; and Thomas Forsyth, United States agent at Fort Armstrong.* Volume 2. (Cleveland, Arthur H. Clarke Company, 1912, 1911 copyright), p.280.

A sermon by the Kickapoo prophet was printed in the *Illinois Monthly Magazine,* of Vandalia, August, 1831, and reprinted in C. C. Tilton, ed., *Centennial Book of Vermilion County,* p. 168,
Illinois (Danville: 1926), pp. 45-46; See also Hiram Beckwith, *History of Vermilion County* (Chicago: H.H. Hill, 1879) and the same author's *Illinois and Indiana Indians,* pp. 117-137.

A. M. Gibson: *The Kickapoos, Lords of the Middle Border* (Norman: University of Oklahoma Press, 1963), pp. 88-90

Joseph B. Herring, *Kenekuk, the Kickapoo Prophet* (Lawrence: University Press of Kansas, 1988).

John Rydjord, *Kansas Place Names* (Norman: University of Oklahoma Press, 1972), p. 434.

F. W. Hodge, ed., *Handbook of the American Indians North of Mexico,* Vol. I, p. 650.

Charles Kappler, *Indian Treaties* (New York: Interland Publishing Co., 1972), pp. 131, 182-184, 366, 636, 839.

Frederick Dockstader, *Great North American Indians* (New York: Van Nostrand Reinhold Company, 1977), pp. 133-134.

Black Partridge (Maw-kaw-be-penay)*
Potawatomi
ca. 1742-1818?

Black Partridge was a younger brother of Waubansee and was a participant in the battle against Anthony Wayne at Fallen Timbers, Ohio, on August 20, 1794. At the treaty of Greenville, August 3, 1795, he received a peace medal bearing the portrait of George Washington. He was chief of a village at the junction of Aux Sable Creek and the Illinois River in La Salle County, Illinois, and later on the Illinois River at the head of Peoria Lake, in Woodford County.

Black Partridge appeared at Fort Dearborn in Chicago on the evening of August 14, 1812, and warned Captain Nathan Heald of impending attack, at the same time returning to him the peace medal he had received in 1795, declaring that since he was unable to restrain his militant warriors, he felt obliged to return it.

Captain Heald had already received orders a week earlier from General William Hull at Detroit, instructing him to abandon the fort and lead his troops, together with a few militia and civilians, to Fort Wayne, Indiana. An escort of thirty Miami under Captain William Wells arrived from Fort Wayne to lead the way. Aside from the escort, the party consisted of fifty-five soldiers, eleven militia, and thirty civilians, including nine women and eighteen children. Meanwhile some five hundred hostile Indians, mostly Potawatomi and some Ottawa under Blackbird, had gathered near the fort. They knew that war had broken out between Britain and the United States and that the British had already captured Mackinac.

As the retreating train of horses and wagons followed the lake shore southward, they were confronted, at about present Eighteenth Street, by the hostile Indians. The Miami fled, but their leader, William Wells, a white man who had been captured as a boy and raised by the Miami, remained to fight and was killed. Captain Heald ordered a charge but was overwhelmed by superior numbers. In a few minutes, fifty-one persons were killed in the retreating party, including three women and twelve children. Black Partridge performed a heroic act by rescuing Mrs. Linai T. Helm, wife of the second in command, by warding off an Indian seeking to tomahawk her, and pulling her into the lake for safety. In 1893 a statue of this event, by Carl Rohl-Smith, was erected at the site, where it stood until 1931. It was then removed to the Chicago Historical Society, where it remains today.

Captain Heald surrendered as soon as he realized his hopeless situation. The prisoners were guaranteed protection, but the promise was not well kept, as thirteen more were killed later. However, the lives of many were saved by the intervention of Black Partridge, Keepotaw, Waubansee, Winnemac, and later, Sauganash (Billy Caldwell), with the help of the Frenchman Antoine Ouilmette and his Potawatomi wife, Archange. A few prisoners, including the Kinzie family, were taken to St. Joseph, Michigan. Others were taken to various Indian villages. Among the latter was Lieutenant Helm, who was wounded in the battle during which his wife was saved by Black Partridge. Some weeks afterward, Black Partridge learned that Lieutenant Helm was a prisoner among Indians on the Kankakee River. After consulting the U.S. agent Thomas Forsyth at Peoria, and being provided with ransom presents, he went to the Kankakee, but in order to obtain the lieutenant's release, he had to add to the ransom a pony, rifle, and gold nose ring. Black Partridge then took Lieutenant Helm to St. Louis, where he was released to Governor William Clark.

Upon returning to his village north of Peoria, Black Partridge found a scene of utter desolation, for an invasion force of three hundred mounted rangers, commanded by Governor Ninian Edwards and Colonel William Russell, had attacked his village and burned it to the ground. The Indians had no warning; most of the men were away on a hunt. The slain victims were mainly women, children, and old people. The caches of corn stored for the winter were burned with everything else, and the ponies were taken away. Soon after, another force led by Captain Thomas E. Craig from Shawneetown ascended the Illinois River in boats, and attacked the largely French settlement at Peoria, burning half the homes and carrying off forty of the inhabitants, as well as some property, including that of Thomas Forsyth. The settlers at Peoria were regarded as allies of the Indians. In 1813 the state began to build Fort Clark at Peoria, which was soon attacked by the enraged Black Partridge.

At Portage des Sioux, in Missouri, on July 18, 1815, Black Partridge signed a peace treaty on behalf of the Potawatomi of Illinois River. His name is there given as Mucketepoke. Thirteen months later, on August 24, 1816, he signed his second and last treaty, in which his name is given as Mucketypokee. In this treaty, the Potawatomi ceded a strip of land twenty miles wide reaching from Lake Michigan to the Illinois River, for about two-and-a-half cents an acre. The strip was wanted for a canal and wagon road. This was the first land cession by the Potawatomi, aside from the six square miles at Chicago which had been ceded at the Treaty of Greenville in 1795. It was only the beginning. By 1833 all Potawatomi land in Illinois had been given up, save for a few small reserves for individuals. Black Partridge did not live to see the end. He died at Peoria Lake soon after the treaty of 1816, although the date is not known.

In his honor, whites named Partridge Creek and Partridge township in Woodford county. In Cook county, southwest of Chicago, near Lemont, his name is on Black Partridge Forest Preserve.

*His Indian name is spelled here as it was in 1899 by the educated Potawatomi Chief Simon Pokagon. See sources.

Sources

Clarence W. Alvord, *The Illinois Country, 1673-1818* (Chicago: Loyola University Press, 1965), pp. 444-445.

Clarence E. Carter, ed., *The Territorial Papers of the United States*, Vols. II-III: *Northwest Territory*, Vols. XVI-XVII: *Illinois Territory* (Washington: U.S. Government Printing Office, 1934-1958).

Charles J. Kappler, ed., *Indian Treaties* (New York: Interland Publishing Co., 1972), pp. 111, 133.

Mrs. John H. Kinzie, *Wau-Bun* (Chicago: Rand McNally Co., 1901), pp. 177-178, 184-185, 192-193.

Nehemiah Matson, *French and Indians of Illinois River*, 2d ed. (Princeton, Illinois: Republican Job Printing Establishment, 1874), pp. 197-209, 245-247.

Simon Pokagon, "The Massacre of Fort Dearborn at Chicago," *Harper's Monthly Magazine*, Vol. 98, No. 586 (March 1899), pp. 649-656.

Milo M. Quaife, *Chicago and the Old Northwest* (Chicago: University of Chicago Press, 1913), pp. 220-221, 415-421.

John Reynolds, *My Own Times* (Chicago: Fergus Printing Co. for Chicago Historical Society, 1879), pp. 87-90, chapter 29.

C. Henry Smith, *Metamora* (Bluffton, Ohio: College Book Shop, 1947), pp. 21-22, 38 ff., 50-51.

Harry L. Spooner, *Indians of Northern Illinois* (Tiskilwa, Illinois: Tiskilwa Chief, 1941), pp. 13-15.

Virgil J. Vogel, *Indian Place Names in Illinois* (Springfield: Illinois State Historical Society, 1963), pp. 14-15, 104.

Billy Caldwell (Sauganash)
Potawatomi (by adoption)
ca. 1780-1841

The best educated Potawatomi of the treaty period was Sauganash (Englishman), or Billy Caldwell. His father was Captain William Caldwell of the British army. His mother was long supposed to be a Potawatomi, but Professor James Clifton recently found evidence that she was a Mohawk. He was born in Canada, where he spent most of his time until 1820. However, he was educated by Jesuit priests at Detroit, and learned both English and French as well as several Indian languages. He was an interpreter and supporter of Tecumseh after 1807, and was also a captain in the Canadian Indian Department. He was in Chicago a few hours after the Fort Dearborn massacre of August 15, 1812, and joined Alexander Robinson in protecting the survivors. He was active in the war on the British side and was probably at the battle of the Thames when Tecumseh was killed.

Caldwell married a Potawatomi, a sister of Yellow Head of the Kankakee River region, and thus became a member of the Potawatomi tribe. He became the father of one son, who died in childhood, and three daughters, Suzanne, born March 27, 1824, Elizabeth, born November 21, 1826, and Helene, born November 29, 1829.

In 1825 Caldwell was recommended for the office of justice of the peace in Chicago, by the Peoria county commissioners, but it is not certain if he received the appointment. He was a registered voter in Chicago in 1826 and 1830.

According to Elijah Haines, who interviewed Alexander Robinson in 1857, Caldwell was elevated to the office of chief, along with Robinson, through the intervention of agent Alexander Wolcott and the French trader Antoine Ouilmette. Their aim was to encourage the adoption of the treaty Prairie du Chien, adopted on July 29, 1829. It involved huge land cessions by the Potawatomi, and rewards for cooperating chiefs. Caldwell was given a lifetime annuity of $600 and a private reserve of two and a half sections along the north branch of the Chicago River, which he sold in 1838. He never lived on the tract, but occupied a frame house that the government built for him on the site of the present Roman Catholic chancery office at Chicago and Wabash avenues. During the Black Hawk War Caldwell earned more gratitude from the government for keeping the Potawatomi neutral For this, and for his activity in behalf of the Chicago treaty of September 26, 1833, which surrendered all remaining tribal land in Illinois and Wisconsin, he received another lifetime annuity of $400, a $600 gift for his three daughters to share, and $5,000 for himself. His name at the end of the treaty is clumsily rendered as Sau-ko-mock. In a supplement signed on October 1, 1834, altering the boundary of the Missouri-Iowa reservation, his name is signed "R. Caldwell." By the Chicago treaty's terms, the Potawatomi moved west within two years. Caldwell went with them, to his credit, and continued to play a leadership role in the west. There he died of cholera on September 28, 1841.

Chicago's first hotel, built by Mark Beaubien in 1829, was called the Sauganash, for the chief. Part of his old reserve on the north branch is in the Cook County Forest Preserve District, and was long called the Sauganash Reserve. Several meaningless names, some honoring local politicians, are now given to various parts of it, but Caldwell Woods and Billy Caldwell golf course are still embraced by the tract. Chicago also has a street, park, public school, and neighborhood called Sauganash, and Caldwell Avenue borders the north side of the old reserve. The south boundary is called Indian Road.

Sources

Clarence A. Burley, "Sauganash," letter of June 13, 1919, to Henry G. Zander. Chicago Historical Society.

Burt E. Burroughs, *Legends and Tales of Homeland on the Kankakee* (Chicago: Regan Publishing House, 1923), pp. 133-139.

Caldwell file, Chicago Historical Society.

James A. Clifton, "Billy Caldwell, Exile in Early Chicago," *Chicago History*, Vol. 6, No. 4 (Winter, 1977-78), pp. 218-228.

James A. Clifton, "Merchant, Soldier, Broker, Chief, A Corrected Obituary of Captain Billy Caldwell," *Journal Illinois State Historical Society*, Vol. 71, No. 3 (August, 1978), pp. 185- 210.

Thomas G. Conway, "An Indian Politician and Entrepreneur in the Old Northwest," *The Old Northwest*, Vol. 1 (March 1975), pp. 51-72.

Dictionary of American Biography (New York: Scribners, 1958-64; 22 volumes), Vol. 8, pp. 376-377.

Lyman Draper, "Tecumseh Manuscripts," Vol. 9, Docs. 27, 65, State Historical Society of Wisconsin.

Ernest E. East, "The Inhabitants of Chicago, 1825-1831," *Journal Illinois State Historical Society*, Vol. 37, No. 2 (June 1944), pp. 131-163.

Elijah M. Haines: *The American Indian (Un-nish-in-na-ba)* (Chicago: The Mas-sin-na-gan Company, 1888), reprint (Evansville: Unigraphic, Inc., 1977), pp. 554-559.

William Hickling and Gurdon S. Hubbard, "Sketches of Billy Caldwell and Shabonee," *Addresses Delivered at Annual Meeting of Chicago Historical Society*, November 19, 1968 (Chicago: Fergus Printing Co., 1882).

George P. Jensen, *Historic Chicago Sites* (Chicago: Creative Enterprises, 1953), pp. 99-102.

Charles J. Kappler, *Indian Treaties* (New York: Interland Publishing Co., 1972), pp. 298, 354, 403, 405, 410, 413, 415.

Mrs. John H. Kinzie, *Wau-Bun* (Chicago: Rand McNally Co., 1901), pp. 187-88.

Juliette Kinzie, "Chicago Indian Chiefs," *Bulletin Chicago Historical Society*, Vol. 1, No. 4 (August, 1935), pp. 108-109.

Cyrus Thomas, "Sagaunash," in F. W. Hodge, Ed: *Handbook of the American Indian North of Mexico*, Vol. 1 (Bureau of Ethnology Bulletin 30, Washington, D.C.: Smithsonian Institution, 1907-1910), Vol. 2, pp. 408-409.

Virgil J. Vogel, *Indian Place Names in Illinois* (Springfield: Illinois State Historical Society, 1962), pp. 16-17, 125-126.

Half Day (Aptakisic)
Potawatomi
1781?-1850?

The oldest post office in Lake County, Illinois, established in 1836, is called Half Day. Nearby are Aptaksic Road, Aptakisic School District, and the tiny village of Aptakisic, established by the Soo Line Railroad in 1888. All these places, and Half Day Road, are named for the same Potawatomi chief, who lived in that vicinity at times in the 1830s. The name Aptakisic literally signifies "center of the sky" or "sun at the meridian," and in two treaties signed by the chief his name is translated as Half Day.

Aptakisic or Half Day was a local band chief and notable orator who signed five treaties between 1827 and 1846. In 1881 John L. Wilson, an early settler, told Wisconsin state historian Lyman Draper that "Op-ta-qu-shick, or Half Day, was the orator of his tribe." He is frequently mentioned in records as a speaker at treaty negotiations and in other meetings with government representatives. His people planted fields near the present site of Half Day, near the junction of Indian Creek and the Des Plaines River, but also camped and hunted along the Du Page River near the present site of Naperville, about thirty miles west of Chicago.

Much of what we know of Half Day is in a nine-page document written in 1893 by Henry W. Blodgett, a lawyer, former state representative and federal judge, who was sixteen years old when he made the acquaintance of Half Day, about 1831. The elder Blodgett was a blacksmith and received frequent visits from Indians in search of repairs for their traps and guns. Young Blodgett befriended the son or grandson of Half Day, who was about his own age. Of Half Day, he later wrote:

> He was good tempered, kind hearted, and generous, a good hunter, and a good provider for his family, and although an inveterate smoker, was very temperate, if not a total abstainer from the use of ardent spirits.

Half Day was probably born in what is now Berrien County, Michigan. It was at St. Joseph, Michigan, that Half Day signed with an "X" his first two treaties, on September 19, 1827, and September 20, 1828. The first treaty involved minor land cessions to remove Indians from the vicinity of the Detroit-Chicago road. The second ceded large chunks of land in southern Michigan, reserving numerous tracts for individuals. Half Day received no benefits from this treaty, and it may have caused him to move to Illinois soon after.

Earlier, Half Day had been an ally of Tecumseh. Blodgett said he was present at the battle of Tippecanoe on November 7, 1811. Half Day was in Michigan when the retreating garrison of Fort Dearborn at Chicago was attacked on August 15, 1812, but said he believed that the Indians were justified. He did participate in the battle of the Thames when Tecumseh was killed, October 5, 1813, and gave Blodgett an account of the affair and Tecumseh's fall. After that defeat, many Indians, including Half Day, were disheartened and deserted the British cause. Soon thereafter, according to Blodgett, Half Day became chief of his band and remained henceforth a friend of the whites.

The village site of Half Day's band and their fields in Lake County were included in territory which was ceded to the government in the treaty of Prairie du Chien, July 29, 1829, but the Indians retained the right to hunt on the ceded land so long as it remained the property of the government. Half Day had no part in this treaty, but many other chiefs received grants of land and cash from that document, which foreshadowed the coming expulsion of the tribe from the Midwest.

When the Black Hawk war began in the spring of 1832, Half Day feared that the few white settlements west of Chicago were in peril. On May 10 he appeared at the Blodgett farm to warn that family and eight others nearby that they should leave at once for the protection of Fort Dearborn at Chicago. The settlers on Du Page River wisely took Half Day's advice and he escorted them by the safest route to Fort Dearborn. At the reconstructed Fort Payne in Naperville, Illinois, there is a painting by Leslie Shrader showing Aptakisic leading the settlers to safety.

Aptakisic and Shabbona joined with the half-blood chiefs, Billy Caldwell and Alexander Robinson, in calling upon the Indian agent at Chicago, Thomas J. V. Owen, to set up a camp at Laughton's Post on the Des Plaines River, about twelve miles from Fort Dearborn, where the more warlike young braves could be kept under surveillance until hostilities ended.

Less than a month after the Fort Armstrong treaty of September 21, 1832, which ended the Black Hawk War, the Potawatomi chiefs received an ungrateful reward when they were called to Tippecanoe River in Indiana to sign away more of their lands in three separate treaties: October 20, October 26, and October 27. Half Day signed the first of these, which ceded an area between Chicago and the Kankakee River. The other two treaties involved land in Indiana and Michigan. The government negotiators seemed to recognize the importance of Half Day when they placed his name first on the treaty of October 20, spelling it Ah-be-te-ke-zhic. For the first and only time he also received a land grant, one square mile on the Kankakee. However, he never occupied it and it was taken from him less than a year later in the treaty at Chicago.

That treaty, on September 27, 1833, was also signed by Half Day. It surrendered all remaining Potawatomi lands in Illinois, Wisconsin, and Michigan, reserving only a few parcels for individuals. Cash payments were made to numerous chiefs and other individuals, but not to Half Day. In return for their homeland the Potawatomi were to receive five million acres in southwestern Iowa and northwestern Missouri, besides several benefits in cash, goods and services. The next year Aptakisic was one of seven individuals who signed treaty amendments giving up the tract in Missouri in exchange for some land on Iowa's Little Sioux River. The Potawatomi living in Illinois were subject to removal immediately after ratification of the treaty, while those in Wisconsin were given three years to leave. After that time, all Indians who wished to receive annuities must have moved west of the Mississippi.

The removal of the greater part of the Illinois Potawatomi took place in 1835, but Half Day, according to Blodgett, did not leave until the Fall of 1837. Meanwhile, in 1835 his band was "coldly denied the exercise of their long cherished custom of making maple sugar in the grove near the settlement."

Blodgett described the chief's despondency as he prepared to move west:

> I well remember the sad face of the old chief as he came to bid our family goodbye. No tears fell from his eyes, but his emotion was as palpable as if he had actually wept, and I know that we all shed tears of genuine sorrow.

In June of 1843 Half Day and other tribal leaders attended a month-long conference of transplanted tribes at Tahlequah, Cherokee Nation, to discuss formation of a loose confederation. Half Day is reported to have spoken frequently and at length, but there was no lasting result from this meeting.

In the fall of 1845 Half Day, Waubansee, and others travelled to Washington for talks with President James K. Polk about proposed terms of a treaty for Potawatomi removal to Kansas. Half Day was a major spokesman, but no documents were signed at that time.

On the site of Council Bluffs, Iowa, on June 5, 1846, Half Day signed his last treaty, in which the Potawatomi surrendered all their lands east of the Missouri River in exchange for a reservation in Kansas only slightly more than one tenth the size of the ceded lands, plus several cash benefits. This reservation, moreover, was to be shared with Potawatomi bands from Indiana which had been living since 1838 on a reservation on Osage River. The Kansas Potawatomi signed their own treaty twelve days later. The Iowa group was to move to Kansas within two years, and most did so.

The last document referring to Half Day that we have been able to learn about is reported by Father Augustin C. Wand, archivist of St. Mary's College, St. Mary's, Kansas. The name of Half Day was among nineteen signatures on a protest to Supt. Thomas Harvey in St. Louis, sent from Soldier's Creek on the Potawatomi reservation, May 30, 1848. It requested that the two schools planned for the reservation be turned over to the Catholic missionaries instead of one to the Baptists and one to the Catholics, as Harvey had recommended.

Since Half Day's name does not appear in the treaty of November 15, 1861, the first signed after that of 1846, it is apparent that he died before that date, but no information on the date of his death has been found. Half Day's story has been cloaked in undeserved obscurity.

Sources

Henry W. Blodgett, "Recollections Concerning Ap-ta-ke-sic (Half Day)," MS, January 23, 1893, in Chicago Historical Society.

_____, *The Autobiography of William Blodgett* (Waukegan: the author, 1906), pp. 21-23, 97.

James Clifton, *Prairie People, Continuity and Change in Potawatomi Indian Culture, 1665-1965* (Lawrence: The Regents Press of Kansas, 1977), pp. 320-322, 329, 338-343.

Lyman C. Draper, ed., "Tecumseh Manuscripts," State Historical Society of Wisconsin, Vol. 9, Doc. 81, November 27, 1881.

R. David Edmunds, "Potawatomis in the Platte Country: An Indian Removal Incomplete," *Missouri Historical Review*, Vol. 68, No. 4 (July, 1974), pp. 375-392.

Gilbert J. Garraghan, *The Jesuits in the Middle United States*, 3 Vols. (New York: America Press, 1938), Vol. 2, p. 620.

Elijah M. Haines: *The American Indian (Un nich in na ba)* (Chicago: The Mas-sin-na-gan Company, 1888), p. 799.

John J. Halsey, *A History of Lake County, Illinois* (Chicago: Roy P. Bates, 1912), p. 545.

Charles J. Kappler, ed., *Indian Treaties* (New York: Interland Publishing Co., 1972), pp. 283-284, 294-300, 353-356, 367-370, 372-375, 402-404, 414-416, 557-560.

Office of Indian Affairs, Letters Received 1824-1881, Chicago Agency, 1824-1834, microcopy M234, Roll. No. 132.

Virgil J. Vogel, *Indian Place Names in Illinois* (Springfield: Illinois State Historical Society, 1962), pp. 11-12, 33.

Virgil J. Vogel, "Half Day, A Forgotten Potawatomi," paper read at American Society for Ethnohistory annual meeting, Chicago, October 11, 1985. Copy in Community Archives of NAES College.

Correspondence, Jane F. Smith, Mary M. Johnson, and Oliver W. Holmes of the National Archives, April 1, 1966, January 3, 1961, and February 11, 1961, respectively; Father Augustin Wand of St. Mary's, Kansas, January 31, 1961, and Prof. James Clifton, of the University of Wisconsin-Green Bay, October, 1985. Held by author.

Menominee
Potawatomi
ca. 1790-1841

Few stories of the Indian removal period carry more pathos than that of Chief Menominee (Wild Rice), leader of a band of Potawatomi at Twin Lakes, Marshall County, Indiana. In the treaty of Tippecanoe, October 26, 1832, twenty-two sections of land were reserved for the bands of Menominee and three other chiefs. In this document, the second and last that he signed, his name is listed as "Min-o-min-ee, his X mark." Less than four years later, at the treaty of Yellow River, August 5, 1836, the government induced the other three chiefs, Pepin-a-waw, No-taw-kah, and Mac-kah-tah-mo-ah, to cede their lands and move west within two years. Their compensation was to be $14,080, from which claims for debts owed to white traders were to be deducted. Menominee firmly refused to sign the treaty. There was no recognition of the fact that his band had, in 1832, been acknowledged as joint owner of the twenty-two sections now being ceded without their consent.

The Indians were aided and advised by their new missionary, Father Benjamin Marie Petit, a young French lawyer-priest who was ordained after his arrival in America. Like his late predecessor, Father Louis Deseille, he told the Indians that if they had not signed the treaty, it was their right to remain on the land. Hundreds of Potawatomi had built their cabins about the mission of Chichipe Outipe (Duck's Head) at Twin Lakes. As devout Catholics, they looked to their priest for guidance. It was the view of Father Deseille that the government's intention toward the Indians was to "extinguish their nationality." Father Petit, who replaced the deceased Louis Deseille in 1837, wrote to Bishop Simon Brute on November 27 of that year that the Indians:

> are preparing to leave for Washington to protest the unworthy manner with which they are treated. The treaty is indeed a thing as illegal as possible and in no wise applicable to our people, who have sold nothing. Menominee, the great chief, another savage, an interpreter, and a lawyer are preparing to leave. It seems to me that if the government has not decided to be completely unjust, they will be listened to.

On December 9, 1837, Father Petit again wrote the bishop, detailing his assistance to the delegation:

> I promised Menominee a memorial, in which I should briefly
> explain their case so that, when he is before the President, he
> may be sure to make them understand the facts with certainty . . .
> . It is a simple, general and logical expose of the facts, tending to
> prove that they did not sign, or that they signed without knowing
> what they were doing, or that some of the signatures appearing
> on the treaty are of people not properly settled on the reserve . . . .
> The reason I promised this to him is that they have so often been
> deceived by lawyers and interpreters, and they have so often been
> made to say what they do not mean, that I am very glad to assure
> them a certain communication of their protests.

The Potawatomi delegation was in Washington by March 3, 1838.
There is no record of their meeting with President Van Buren aside
from the report by J. T. Douglass of Menominee's statement "that
when at Washington last week he heard the president say, that no
white men had any right to come upon their land until they had ceded
it to the Government."

Whatever the president said, other officials, both in the capital and
in Indiana, gave the Indians no hope. On April 4, 1838, Father Petit
wrote to his family:

> I now face the sad prospect of my Indian mission's early destruc-
> tion .... I began however to feel more resigned. A trip to Washing-
> ton, with pressing protestations to the President, has been with-
> out effect.

On July 26 he described events in a report to his bishop:

> First, to give you a report of the trip to Washington: it was use-
> less. "I do not wish to speak of it," said the President. "Your
> names are on the treaty; your lands are lost," said the Secretary
> of War [Joel R. Poinsett]. "But here is one of the witnesses to the
> treaty who will show you how everything was a fraud." "I do not
> need to be shown, and we did not need your signatures: the great
> chiefs of the nation were entitled to sell your reserve."

Petit added that it was the opinion of lawyers that the case could
not be pleaded before the federal courts because the government
refused to permit itself to be sued and no jury was possible.

A few days before this letter, on July 17 and 18, a council with
Superintendent Abel C. Pepper and others was held at Menominee's
reserve. There Pepper warned the Indians that their refusal to move
would violate the treaty and cause the use of force against them.
Father Petit reported also on this meeting, and the stand taken by
Menominee. The chief maintained that the president was unaware of

the truth concerning the treaty. Reportedly he asserted:

> He does not know that your treaty is a lie, and that I never signed
> it. He does not know that you [Pepper] made my young chiefs
> drunk and got their consent and pretended to get mine. He does
> not know that I have refused to sell my lands and still refuse. He
> would not by force drive me from my home, and the graves of my
> tribe, and my children who have gone to the Great Spirit, nor
> allow you to tell me your braves will take me, tied like a dog, if he
> knows the truth. My brothers, the President is just, but he listens
> to the word of the young chiefs who have lied; and when he knows
> the truth he will leave me to my own. I have not sold my lands. I
> will not sell them. I have not signed any treaty and will not sign
> any. I am not going to leave my lands, and I don't want to hear
> anything more about it. (Irving McKee, ed., *The Trail of Death,
> Letters of Benjamin Marie Petit* [Indianapolis: Indiana Historical
> Society, 1941], p. 82.)

The childlike faith of Menominee in the righteousness of Van
Buren reveals a naivete about the chain of command in government,
and a lack of awareness that Van Buren's policy in all respects was a
continuation of that of Jackson. It is a cause for wonder that Van
Buren, who ran for president on an anti-slavery ticket ten years later,
could show such a calloused attitude toward the Indians.

Meanwhile some minor violence erupted as whites, intent on pre-
emption, began to occupy Indian land. A hundred volunteers were
raised who interned some Indians and burned a dozen of their cabins.
Indians were forcibly rounded up for deportation. On the day of
departure, September 4, 859 of them had been assembled. By one
report, Menominee had to be lassoed, bound hand and foot, and
thrown into a wagon. (Jacob Piatt Dunn, *True Indian Stories* [Indian-
apolis: Sentinel Printing Co., 1909], p. 49.) The encampment was
levelled by fire and some rebellious chiefs were placed in a cage that
followed the flag. The line of coaches, wagons, horses, people on foot,
and soldiers formed a line almost three miles long.

Father Petit did not at first accompany the Indians, although he
joined them later. Only ten days after their departure, he wrote:

> We learned that the Indians on the way, with bayonets prodding
> their backs, had a large number of sick in their ranks—that sev-
> eral, crammed into baggage wagons, had already died of heat and
> thirst.

On September 9, physicians who visited the emigrants near
Logansport, Indiana, found about three hundred of them sick. By that
evening five children had died. On September 17, Father Petit joined

the party at Danville, Illinois. In a letter of September 23 he reported that "intermittent fever" (malaria) was rampant not only among the Indians, but in white communities along the way. The priest himself soon caught the disease. More deaths were reported in his letters, and almost daily in the journal of the emigration conductor, William Polke. Children and the aged were the principal victims.

After leaving the heat, dust, and water-scarce prairies, the party ran into cold, snow, and rain in Missouri. They arrived at Osage River in the future state of Kansas on November 4. On November 13 Father Petit sent a detailed report of the journey to Bishop Brute. He reported that the heat had been excessive, the weather sultry, and the water bad. After crossing the Mississippi the sickness began to decline. By the end of the trip, forty-three deaths were officially recorded, and about a hundred desertions.

Although ill, Father Petit began his trip back to Indiana in the winter. On January 15, 1839, he reached St. Louis, where he was compelled to stop and accept the care of the Jesuits. He died on February 10, 1839, aged twenty-eight. His journals and letters constitute our principal record of the last months of Menominee's band in Indiana and of their migration to the west.

There is no known record of the birth date of Chief Menominee. The end of his life, however, is recorded at St. Mary's mission in Kansas, with the notation: "Died, on 15 April, 1841. Alexis Menominee," with the additional comment that he was aged about fifty and was buried the same day. In 1909, by state appropriations and private donations, a monument was dedicated to the memory of Menominee at Twin Lakes, southwest of Plymouth, Indiana. The inscription reads: "In memory of Menominee and his band of 859 Potawatomi Indians, removed from the reservation, September 4, 1838, by a company of soldiers under General John Tipton, authorized by Governor David Wallace." The statue shows the chief in a combination of Indian and white man's clothing, topped by a Sioux headdress.

Menominee deserves to be remembered as one of the few chiefs who held out to the end against all efforts to uproot his people from their beloved homeland.

Sources

Jacob Piatt Dunn, *True Indian Stories* (Indianapolis: Sentinel Printing Co., 1909, reprint Manchester, Indiana: L. W. Schultz, 1964), pp. 234-252.

Charles J. Kappler, ed., *Indian Treaties* (New York: Interland Publishing Co., 1972), pp. 367-369, 462-463.

Larry L. Leach, "Final Journey," *Indiana History Bulletin*, Vol. 52 (April 1975), pp. 43-44.

Donald McDonald, *Removal of the Potawattomies from Northern Indiana* (Plymouth, Indiana: D. McDonald & Co., 1899).

Irving McKee, "The Centennial of 'The Trail of Death,'" *Indiana Magazine of History*, Vol. 35, No. 1 (March 1939), pp. 27-48.

Irving McKee, ed., *The Trail of Death, Letters of Benjamin Marie Petit* (Indianapolis: Indiana Historical Society, 1941).

William Polke, "Journal of an Emigrating Party of Potawattomie Indians...," *Indiana Magazine of History*, Vol. 21, No. 4 (December 1925), pp. 316-336.

Dwight Smith, ed., "A Continuation of the Journal of an Emigrating Party of Potawatomi Indians, 1838, and Ten William Polke Manuscripts," *Indiana Magazine of History*, Vol. 44, No. 4 (December 1948), pp. 393-408.

Benjamin F. Stuart, "The Deportation of Menominee and his Tribe of Potawattomie Indians," *Indiana Magazine of History*, Vol. 18, No. 3 (September 1922), pp. 255-265.

Otto Winger, *The Potawatomi Indians* (Elgin, Illinois: Elgin Press, 1939), pp. 43-54.

Monee
Ottawa
1783-1866

About 1795, a twenty-one-year-old Quebec-born Frenchman named Joseph Bailly (1774-1835) came to trade among the Potawatomi Indians about the St. Joseph River, in southwestern Michigan. He first married a Potawatomi woman, from whom he separated in 1810. He next married a French-Ottawa mixed blood, Marie Le Fevre, widow of a Frenchman, and in 1822 settled on the Little Calumet River in northwestern Indiana. This was in Potawatomi territory near the site of present Chesterton. The Potawatomi, lacking an *r* sound, had difficulty pronouncing the name of Marie, so they called her Maunee or Monee.

Bailly's second wife, Marie (1783-1866), bore him two sons and six daughters. The first son died in infancy, and the second, Robert, died of typhoid fever while attending the Cary mission school conducted by Rev. Isaac McCoy, a Baptist, at Niles, Michigan. Although the Baillys were Catholic, they sent some of their children to the nearest available school. The girls were eventually educated in Detroit and in Canada. According to Frances Howe, granddaughter of Monee, only four of the daughters reached maturity.

Bailly did a flourishing fur trade in Indiana, and was favorably situated on the road from Detroit to Chicago. At that time it was free of white settlement. The well-known travel chronicler, Charles Fenno Hoffman, was once a visitor at the Bailly home. (Charles Fenno Hoffman, *A Winter in the West*, 2 Vols. [Ann Arbor: University Microfilms, 1966], Vol. 1, p. 230.)

The treaty of Tippecanoe, Indiana, October 20, 1832, awarded "For the five daughters of Mo-nee, by her last husband, Joseph Bailey, two sections" of land. Another treaty at the same place six days later gave one section to "Tou-se-qua the wife of Joe Baily." This contradicts the statement made by Francis Howe, in a letter to Robert Fergus on April 22, 1884, that her grandmother had no Indian name.

In the treaty of Chicago, September 26, 1833, a cash gift of $500 was to be shared by Esther, Rosene, and Eleanor Bailly, daughters of Monee, while Sophia, Hortense, and Theresa Bailly shared $1,000. Sophia and Theresa must have been minors, for they are not among the four listed by Frances Howe as reaching maturity. This treaty also allowed $500 for Robert and Esther, "son and daughter of Joseph Dailly." This was probably a clerk's error for Bailly. According to Winger, however, Robert died six years earlier, in 1827. Moreover, Theresa already had a share in the $500 already granted to her and her sisters Sophia and Hortense. Finally, the father, Joseph Bailly, was given $4,000, undoubtedly for using his influence to gain Indian consent to a treaty which provided for Potawatomi removal from Illinois.

Today the Bailly homestead, with its restored buildings and family cemetery, are part of the Indiana Dunes National Lakeshore, and open to visitors. Nearby, on U.S. highway #12, the village of Baileytown commemorates the former proprietor of the land. It was once the site of an intended nuclear power plant, on which construction was terminated in 1981. Monee is commemorated today by the town of Monee, on the Illinois Central Railroad in Will county, Illinois.

Sources

William K. Ackerman, *Early Illinois Railroads* (Chicago: Fergus Printing Co., 1884), pp. 120-123; contains letter from Frances R. Howe.

Joseph O. Bowers, *The Old Bailly Homestead* (Gary, Indiana, 1922).

Elijah M. Haines, *The American Indian* (*Un-nish-in-na-ba*) (Chicago: The Mas-sin-na-gan Company, 1888), p. 755.

Frances Rose Howe, *The Story of a French Homestead in the Old Northwest* (Columbus, 1907).

Charles J. Kappler, *Indian Treaties* (New York: Interland Publishing Co., 1972), pp. 353, 374, 405-406.

Martha Miller, *Dunes Settler* (Chesterton, Indiana: Miller Publications, 1980).

Powell A. Moore, *The Calumet Region, Indiana's Last Frontier* (Indianapolis: Indiana Historical Bureau, 1959).

Virgil J. Vogel, *Indian Place Names in Illinois* (Springfield: Illinois State Historical Society, 1962), pp. 80-81.

Otho Winger, *The Potawatomi Indians* (Elgin, Illinois: Elgin Press, 1939), pp. 119-121.

Archange Ouilmette
Potawatomi
1764-1840

On the shore of Lake Michigan fourteen miles north of Chicago's Loop is an affluent suburb which was incorporated in 1872 as the village of Wilmette, a designation it still retains, although its population a century later reached 32,134. The name it bears is an anglicized spelling of the French name Ouilmette, and was given to the settlement at the suggestion of Judge Henry Blodgett of Waukegan, in honor of a Potawatomi Indian woman, Archange Ouilmette. She acquired the surname by her marriage in 1796 or 1797 to Antoine Ouilmette, a French Canadian fur trader and farmer who settled at Chicago in 1790, in his thirtieth year. Without doubt, he was the first white settler on the site of the future metropolis, though he was preceded by a black man, Jean Baptiste Pointe du Sable. Ouilmette had his cabin where the Tribune tower now stands, and for a time was employed by the American Fur Company. Later he worked for John Kinzie, a trader who came to Chicago in 1803, the year that Fort Dearborn was built at what is now the southwest corner of Michigan Avenue and Wacker Drive.

Archange, born in 1764 at Sugar Creek, Michigan, was probably the daughter of Francois Chevalier, a mixed-blood Potawatomi of some prominence who lived at St. Joseph, Michigan, and his half-blood wife, May Ann. Although Ouilmette's grandson, I. J. Martell, in 1905 told Frank Grover that Francois Chevalier was a white man, the evidence indicates otherwise. The information came from his mother Sophia, whose memory may have been impaired, since she was then eighty-eight years old. Francois Chevalier was a Potawatomi signer of the Treaty of Tippecanoe, October 20, 1832, although a clerk spelled his name "Francois Cho-van-ier." In the text of the treaty, "Sho-bon-ier or Chevalier" was awarded $40 for a stolen horse, and "Francois Sho-bon-ier" was to receive $120 for three horses lost in the Black Hawk War. It is probable that the last named was the son of the first.

Catherine, the daughter of one Francois Chevalier, probably the junior one, married the half-blood Potawatomi Alexander Robinson (Che-Che-Pinqua), who was appointed a chief for treaty purposes, with the connivance of Antoine Ouilmette, at Prairie du Chien, Wisconsin, in July, 1829.

After the massacre of the retreating garrison of Fort Dearborn by the Potawatomi, on August 15, 1812, the Ouilmettes helped disguise and save two survivors, Mrs. Margaret Helm and a soldier named Griffin. A Frenchman was usually safe on the frontier, so Ouilmette remained at his home, and was for the next four years the only white resident of Chicago.

The fort was rebuilt and the little village of Chicago began again in 1816. Ouilmette, although illiterate, was enough of a solid citizen to pay a tax of $4 in 1825 on property valued at $400. He is also recorded as a voter in 1826, and in 1833, though he had left the city, and signed a petition to the Catholic bishop of St. Louis asking that a parish be established in Chicago. In 1826 or soon thereafter, Ouilmette built a cabin of hewn logs for his wife and family of eight children near Gross Point. That is the site of the lighthouse at the foot of Evanston's Central Avenue, but early settlers said his cabin was at the foot of Lake Avenue in Wilmette. A description of the five million acres of land ceded by the Potawatomis at the treaty of Prairie du Chien in 1829 reads: "Beginning on the western shore of Lake Michigan, at the northeast corner of the field of Antoine Ouilmette, who lives near Gross Point, about twelve (12) miles north from Chicago ..."

The Chicago Indian agent, Dr. Alexander Wolcott, recognizing Ouilmette's influence with the Indians, sent him to aid the treaty commissioners in persuading the Potawatomi to surrender the bulk of their lands in Illinois and Wisconsin. Because he was a white man, the Senate by custom would not ratify a treaty which awarded him land in payment for services rendered, so the usual device was employed, of giving grants to his wife and children, who qualified as Indians. Therefore, Article 4 of the treaty reads:

> To Archange Ouilmette, a Potawatomi woman, wife of Antoine, two sections of land for herself and her children on Lake Michigan, south of and adjoining the northern boundary of the cession herein made by Indians aforesaid to the United States.

Residents of the North Shore, as this region is now called, will be interested in knowing that the boundaries of this reserve, as eventually surveyed, included three hundred acres in Evanston and nine hundred and eighty acres in Wilmette.

Four years later, in a treaty signed at Chicago on September 26, 1833, the Potawatomi ceded all their remaining tribal lands in Illinois and agreed to move within two years to a reservation in western Iowa. This time Ouilmette was able to get some cash, $800 for himself for "claims admitted to be justly due," (but not specified), and a total of $1,859 for family members, including an adopted daughter and her children.

The Ouilmettes were the parents of eight children, whose names were Joseph, Mitchell, Louis, Francis, Elizabeth, Archange, Sophia, and Josette, besides an adopted daughter, Archange Trombla. Of these, Sophia was still living in 1905 and furnished, through her son I. J. Martell, information on family history which was published by Frank Grover of Evanston, and which has been relied upon for some facts in this sketch. Sophia died near St. Mary's, Kansas, March 27, 1911, aged ninety-four. From the birth of Antoine Ouilmette to the death of his last child is a span of 151 years.

The Ouilmettes lived on their reservation until 1838. In 1839 Antoine, at least, was on the farm near Racine, Wisconsin, where his son Joseph had settled in 1834. By 1840, all of the Ouilmette children except Joseph and Josette had migrated to the Iowa reservation, and it was there that Archange Ouilmette died on November 25, 1840, at age seventy-six. Her husband followed her, aged eighty-one, on December 1, 1841.

The now unoccupied Ouilmette reserve, meanwhile, was being plundered of its main resource, standing timber, by white neighbors. According to treaty it could not be sold without permission of the president. On February 22, 1844, seven of the Ouilmette children petitioned President John Tyler for permission to sell the reserve. According to Grover, the south half, six hundred forty acres, was sold to a land company for $1,000, a little over $1.50 an acre, while the north half was sold in separate parcels for a larger, but unstated, sum. Joseph, the only child who did not sign the petition, received a one-hundred- sixty-acre parcel of the land and made his own sale for $460. After farming a few more years near Wausau, Wisconsin, Joseph joined his brothers and sisters on the Potawatomi reservation, which by that time, following another treaty, was located in Kansas.

A portrait of Archange Ouilmette, as conceived by the artist George Lusk, hangs in the Wilmette village hall with a copy in possession of the Wilmette Historical Museum. Her image was copied from it for a centennial souvenir tile in 1972. The costume and jewelry, however, resemble that of a gypsy more than that of an Indian.

Besides being given to a village, the name of Wilmette was perpetuated in another way. On July 24, 1915, the excursion steamboat *Eastland* overturned in the Chicago River, with a loss of 815 lives, making it the greatest marine disaster in the history of the Great Lakes. The *Eastland* was raised and remodeled as a training ship for the U.S. Navy, and rechristened *U.S.S. Wilmette*. After being used to train seamen in two world wars, the 275-foot craft was scrapped in 1946. Somehow, the fate of this boat seems to parallel that of the family for which it was named.

Sources

A. T. Andreas, *A History of Chicago*, 2 Vols. (Chicago: A. T. Andreas, 1884), Vol. 1, p. 48.

George D. Bushnell, *Wilmette: A History* (Wilmette: Wilmette Bicentennial Commission, 1976), *passim*.

Ernest E. East, "The Inhabitants of Chicago, 1825-1831," *Journal Illinois State Historical Society*. Vol. 37, No. 2, (June, 1944) pp. 131-163, p. 135.

Weston A. Goodspeed and Daniel D. Healey, *History of Cook County, Illinois*, 2 Vols. (Chicago: the Goodspeed Historical Association, 1909), Vol. 2, p. 267.

Frank R. Grover, *Antoine Ouilmette* (Evanston, Illinois: Evanston Historical Society, 1908), *passim*.

Elijah M. Haines: *The American Indian (Un-nish-in-na-ba)* (Chicago: The Mas-sin-na-gan Company, 1888), pp. 554-557.

Harry Hansen, *The Chicago* (New York: Farrar & Rinehart, 1942), pp. 246-252.

George Jensen, *Historic Chicago Sites* (Chicago: Creative Enterprises, 1953), pp. 25-28.

Charles Kappler, *Indian Treaties* (New York: Interland Publishing Co., 1972), pp. 298, 353-355, 405, 408.

Virgil J. Vogel, *Indian Place Names in Illinois* (Springfield: Illinois State Historical Society, 1962), pp. 167-168.

Letter from Verschelder Funeral Home, St. Mary's, Kansas, to Wilmette Historical Society, April 7, 1965, typescripts on the history of Wilmette in files of Wilmette Historical Society.

Thanks are due to Eileen Drumm, director of the Wilmette Historical Museum, who opened the museum files for examination.

Alexander Robinson (Che-Che-Pinqua)
Potawatomi
1789-1872

The only Potawatomi chief of the immediate Chicago area who failed to go west to Iowa with his people in 1835 was Alexander Robinson or Che-Che-Pinqua (Blinking Eye or Squint Eye). By his own account, given to Lyman Draper in 1866, Robinson was born at Mackinaw, Michigan, in 1789, the son of a Scottish trader and an Ottawa Indian mother. At the age of five he is supposed to have witnessed the battle of Fallen Timbers, near Toledo, Ohio, between allied Indian tribes and troops commanded by Gen. Anthony Wayne. As a young man Robinson took up residence with the Potawatomi about St. Joseph, Michigan.

When Indians attacked the Ft. Dearborn garrison and their civilian entourage at 18th street and the lake front on August 15, 1812, Robinson was reported paddling along the south shore of Lake Michigan toward Chicago. Upon being warned by some friendly Miami not to go there, he made camp at the mouth of Calumet River and remained there for a time.

Mrs. Margaret Helm, whose husband, Lieutenant Helm, died in the massacre, was taken to St. Joseph and sheltered there. Later, Capt. Nathan Heald and his wife Rebecca, who had survived the battle, were at their request paddled three hundred miles to Mackinaw by Alexander Robinson, who turned them over to the British for their own safety.

In 1814 Robinson became a permanent resident of Chicago, joining with Antoine Ouilmette (Wilmette) in cultivating the gardens of the deserted fort. In 1826 he was married at Chicago to Catherine Chevalier, daughter of a prominent half-blood of St. Joseph and thus became formally a member of the Potawatomi tribe.* The ceremony was performed by justice of the peace John Kinzie, Chicago's first white American settler. At the treaty of Prairie du Chien on July 29, 1829, where the Potawatomi made large cessions of land, the government reserved for Robinson two square miles of land along the Des Plaines River, centered at present Lawrence Avenue. This was given as a reward for assisting in winning Indian acceptance of the treaty. He also received a lifetime annuity of $200.

In the treaty of Tippecanoe, Indiana, October 20, 1832 Robinson received another lifetime annuity of $200, and in the treaty of Chicago, September 27, 1833, a third lifetime annuity of $300, besides $5,000 in cash.

During the Winnebago scare of 1827, Robinson helped keep the

Potawatomi at peace. Again during the Black Hawk War in the late spring and summer of 1832, Robinson was a volunteer in one of the companies of militia raised at Chicago, which occupied Fort Dearborn temporarily. Robinson joined with Billy Caldwell in keeping Potawatomi braves quietly encamped at Laughton's post on the Des Plaines River.

According to Elijah Haines, one time speaker of the Illinois House of Representatives, who interviewed Robinson in 1857, Caldwell and Robinson were both elevated to the imaginary title of chief of the united Potawatomi, Ottawa, and Chippewa at the Prairie du Chien treaty in 1829. This move was arranged by agent Alexander Wolcott, with the aid of Antoine Ouilmette, because these two leaders were influential in securing Indian land cessions, preparatory to removal.

Robinson, a resident of Chicago, was assessed on personal property of $200 in 1825. This may have been his cabin at Hardscrabble, formerly Lee's place, at Racine Avenue and the South branch. In 1823 and 1826 he was employed as an interpreter for Alexander Wolcott, at a salary of $365. He was recorded as a voter in 1826 and 1830, and in 1830 was licensed to keep a tavern in Chicago. This place stood at Canal and Lake streets, at the fork of the Chicago River. It was closed in 1835, when the Potawatomi left Illinois, and Robinson, by one account, lived three years in Du Page County before settling on his Des Plaines River reservation. There he lived until his death on April 22, 1872. He was preceded in death by his wife, on August 7, 1860, and seven of his fourteen children. Their family burial plot beside their home once had markers for each burial, but these were removed, allegedly because of vandalism, in the 1940s, and replaced by a single quartzite marker, by action of the forest preserve district.

Robinson's granddaughter, Mrs. Katherine Boettcher, born in 1866, continued to live in the Robinson home, a two story frame structure, in the forest preserve near Lawrence Avenue and East River Road, together with her son Herbert, until the house burned down on May 25, 1955. When Herbert died on July 3, 1973, permission for him to be buried in the family plot was refused by the forest preserve district.

Robinson's Woods and Che-Che-Pinqua Woods in the Cook County Forest Preserve District memorialize the chief's European and aboriginal names, while Catherine Chevalier Woods commemorates his wife. All three tracts are within the bounds of the former reservation.

The life of Chief Robinson encompassed changes which in the Old World took thousands of years. He was born in an Indian village barely out of the stone age, in the same year that George Washington was inaugurated as first president of the United States, and died during the administration of U.S. Grant. He settled at Chicago when it was inhabited by only one French Potawatomi family. He signed three treaties with the U.S. government, surrendering an empire. He saw his tribe go sorrowfully toward the west, but remained behind to see Chicago grow to a metropolis of hundreds of thousands of people. He saw men march off to the Civil War, saw the coming of the telegraph, steamship, and railroad. He saw much of the great metropolis burn to the ground in 1871, and watched it rise again from the ashes, before his long life finally closed in 1872. Perhaps never again will any man see so much change in one lifetime.

*The Robinsons had been united by Indian custom some time before 1812.

Sources

A. T. Andreas, *History of Cook County, Illinois* (Chicago: A. T. Andreas, 1884), pp. 108, 880.

Chicago Sun-Times, July 5, 1973, p. 36.

Chicago Tribune, May 26, 1955.

Lyman W. Draper, "Notes," in "Tecumseh Manuscripts," Vol. S-21 (interview with Chief Robinson *et al.*), 1866, State Historical Society of Wisconsin, p. 288.

M. L. Dunlap, "Chief Robinson of the Potawatomies," *Chicago Illustrated Journal*, March 1873, pp. 46-47.

Ernest E. East, "The Inhabitants of Chicago, 1825-1831," *Journal of the Illinois State Historical Society*, June 1944, pp. 156-157.

Louise Houghton, *Our Debt to the Red Man* (Boston: The Stratford Co., 1918), p. 107.

Elijah M. Haines: *The American Indian (Un-nish-in-na-ba)* (Chicago: The Mas-sin-na-gan Company, 1888), pp 554-559.

George P. Jensen, *Historic Chicago Sites* (Chicago: Creative Enterprises, 1953), pp. 55-57.

Charles Kappler, *Indian Treaties* (New York: Interland Publishing Co., 1972), pp. 298-99, 356, 403, 410, 413, 415.

Mrs. John H. (Juliette) Kinzie, *Wau-Bun* (Chicago: Rand McNally Co., 1901), pp. 191, 200.

"Chicago Indian Chiefs" (letter to Lyman Draper, June 20, 1866), *Bulletin of the Chicago Historical Society*, August, 1935, pp. 108-109.

Virgil J. Vogel, *Indian Place Names in Illinois* (Springfield: Illinois State Historical Society, 1962), pp. 21-22, 119.

Shabbona
Potawatomi
1775-1859

Shabbona, like several other Potawatomi leaders, entered the tribe through marriage, after the War of 1812. Reports of the place of his birth are contradictory, although, according to one report, Shabbona said he was born on the Maumee River in Ohio. His father was an Ottawa, by all accounts, while his mother, according to Juliette Kinzie, was a Seneca. He was said to be a nephew of Tecumseh, a grand-nephew of Pontiac, and on his mother's side an uncle of the Ottawa writer Andrew J. Blackbird.

Shabbona fought in the battle of Tippecanoe, November 7, 1811, and when war with Great Britain broke out the next year, he followed Tecumseh into the British service. He took part in the Battle of River Raisin near Detroit, but when Tecumseh was killed at Chatham, Ontario, on October 5, 1813, the Indians accused the British of cowardice, and Shabbona transferred his allegiance to the Americans.

After the war he was given a certificate for his British service, signed by Capt. Billy Caldwell, who was destined to become an important Potawatomi chief. Shabbona settled at the Pawpaw Grove in De Kalb county, Illinois, and while there became a Potawatomi peace chief. He signed his first treaty at St. Louis on August 24, 1816, ceding to the United States a strip of land twenty miles wide reaching from Lake Michigan to the Illinois River. This strip was intended to facilitate the building of a road and a canal, which was begun in 1836 and finished in 1848. Shabbona, like the others, signed the treaty with an "X" but the clerk wrote his name as Chamblee, one of sixteen forms of his name which can be found in documents. In the first treaty of Prairie du Chien, August 19, 1825, which established tribal boundaries, he is listed as an Ottawa, and his name is written "Chaboner or Chambly." In all other treaties that he signed, he is listed as a Potawatomi. In the second treaty of Prairie du Chien, July 29, 1829, a clause reads "for Shab-eh-nay, two sections at his village near Pawpaw grove." In a treaty signed at Tippecanoe, Indiana, on October 20, 1832, his name is given as Shab-e-neai. In the treaty at Chicago, September 26, 1833, the last signed by the Potawatomi in Illinois, they gave up all their Illinois land in return for a reservation along the Missouri River about the site of present Council Bluffs, Iowa, and pledged to move there within two years. This treaty gave to "Shabehnay" a lifetime annuity of $200.

During the Winnebago scare of 1827, sometimes miscalled an "Uprising," Shabbona joined the Potawatomi leading men in maintaining neutrality. To that end, in the company of Billy Caldwell, he made a perilous trip to Big Foot's village at Lake Geneva, Wisconsin. Again, when the Sauk under Black Hawk became embroiled in war in 1832, Shabbona not only preached peace, but also joined his son in a night ride to warn settlers to seek safety from impending attack by going to Ottawa. A number of people assembled at the Davis farm on Indian Creek near present Harding, Illinois, did not heed his warning, and fifteen of them were killed May 21, 1832, by a band of Potawatomi in sympathy with Black Hawk. The site of this event, in La Salle county, is now called Shabbona Park. There one may see monuments commemorating both the victims and their would-be rescuer. In later years Shabbona was punished for his activity when hostile Indians killed one of his sons and a nephew.

In 1836 Shabbona went west to visit his tribe in Iowa, but soon returned to his grove. During another visit to the Potawatomi after their removal to Kansas in 1848, Shabbona's land was declared abandoned and was sold to a settler. When Shabbona returned he was beaten with a stick and driven off by the new owner.

With his two wives and several children, the homeless chief retired to the Illinois River where white friends bought him twenty acres near the mouth of the Mazon. Here he lived in a cabin until his death on July 27, 1859. He was buried in Evergreen Cemetery at Morris, where his grave is marked by a granite boulder bearing only this inscription: "Shabbona 1775-1859." His residence in De Kalb county is commemorated by the names of the village and township of Shabbona, and by another village and a forest preserve called Shabbona Grove. At Shabbona a stylized and unrealistic statue of the chief stands in front of the high school bearing his name. Elsewhere he is memorialized by the name of Shabonee school in Northbrook, Illinois, Shabbona Woods in the Cook County Forest Preserves, Shabbona Park in Chicago, and by the village of Shabbona in Sanilac county, Michigan. In the Johnson Mound Forest Preserve of Kane county, Illinois, stands the Shabbona Elm, dedicated to the chief's memory.

The name Shabbona is pronounced with the accent on the first syllable. Its spelling varies, as does its interpretation. The view that it signifies "built like a bear" cannot be reconciled with Indian vocabularies. Juliette Kinzie held that his name was corrupted from French Chambly, from Champ-de-ble, "field of wheat," which is a place name in Quebec and also a personal name. One view holds that he was named for a Jacques de Chambly. French origin of the name was denied by Shabbona's grand niece, Frances R. Howe. Shabbona is sometimes confused with Shobonier, but both names are found in the first treaty of Tippecanoe, October 20, 1832, and the treaty of Chicago. The first of these makes the separate identity of Shobonier clear by awarding forty dollars for a stolen horse to "Shobonier, or Cheva-lier," and listing "Shab-e- neai" among the signers. Clearly Shobonier is a corruption of Chevalier, the name of a notable French-Potawa-tomi family of St. Joseph, Michigan.

Sources

Andrew J. Blackbird, *History of the Ottawa and Chippewa Indians* (Ypsilanti, Michigan: Ypsilanti Job Printing House, 1887, reprint, 1977).

F. W. Hodge, ed., *Handbook of the American Indian North of Mexico*, Vol. 2, (Bureau of Ethnology Bulletin 30, Washington, D.C.: Smithsonian Institution, 1907-1910) pp. 517-518.

Frances R. Howe to Lyman Draper, Sept. 29, 1888, "Tecumseh Manuscript," State Historical Society of Wisconsin, Vol. 9, Doc. 86, also P. A. Armstrong in Doc. 76.

Charles Kappler, *Indian Treaties* (New York: Interland Publishing Co., 1972), pp. 133, 298, 354, 404, 410, 560.

Juliette A. Kinzie, "Chicago Indian Chiefs," *Bulletin Chicago Historical Society*, Vol. 1, No. 4 (August 1935); letter to Draper, June 20, 1866, pp. 109-10.

Nehemiah Matson, *Memories of Shaubena*, 2d ed. (Chicago: Donnelley, Cassette and Lloyd, 1880).

Wayne C. Temple, *Shabbona, Friend of the Whites* (Springfield: Illinois State Museum, 1957).

Horace Greeley Smith, "The Midnight Ride of a Potawatamie Chief," typescript, 5 pp., Rock River conference of Methodist church, n.d., courtesy Rev. Jack Cory, Northbrook, Illinois. Held by author.

Mrs. Alta P. Walters, "Shabonee," *Journal of Illinois State Historical Society*, Vol. 17 (October 1924), pp. 381-397.

B.L. Wick, "Shabbona and the Part He Played in the Pioneer History of the Mississippi Valley," *Annals of Iowa*, 3d series, Vol. 17, No. 3 (January, 1930), pp. 168-172.

Waubansee
Potawatomi
1765?-1848?

Waubansee (Waubonsee, Waubonsie, etc.) was probably born about
1765 near the head of the Kankakee River in St. Joseph County, Indiana, although some writers, less credibly, have placed his birth date
in 1747 or in 1756. According to J. N. Bourassa, he was a younger
brother of Black Partridge. Little is known of his early life, and much
of the information about him is mythical or contradictory. At some
point he attained the title of a war chief of the Potawatomi. He participated in the attack on the retreating Ft. Dearborn garrison at Chicago, August 15, 1812, but is reported to have guarded the Kinzie
family afterwards. Following the War of 1812, he never again participated in any action against white settlers or troops. He signed his
first treaty at St. Louis, August 24, 1816, wherein his name is listed
as Wapunsy. In six other treaties and one treaty supplement that he
signed, up to 1834, his name appears as Wa-ban-see, Wau-pon- eh-
see, Wah-ponsch, Wah-pou-seh, Wah-bou-seh, and Wau-bon-see.
Since he could not write, his name was written by treaty clerks as it
sounded to them. Herein we spell his name as it is spelled by his fifth
generation descendant, A. John Waubansee of La Crosse, Wisconsin.

Waubansee was neutral during the Winnebago troubles of 1827,
and campaigned with the Illinois militia in the Black Hawk War of
1832. For his various services the treaty of Prairie du Chien on July
29, 1829, reserved for him "five sections of land at the Grand Bois, on
Fox River of the Illinois." Three years later the treaty of Tippecanoe,
Indiana, October 20, 1832, awarded him five sections (square miles)
"in the Prairie near Rock Village" (on the Kankakee).

Waubansee settled in the Grand Bois, or "Big Woods," below
Aurora, on the Fox River, sometime in the 1820s. In 1828 his village
at that place had a population of 51 persons. It was visited by Juliette
Kinzie in 1831 and mentioned in *Wau-Bun.*

In 1835 Waubansee migrated west with his tribe to the reservation
in southwestern Iowa near the site of present Council Bluffs.
Accounts of him after that date are often unreliable. He visited Washington on tribal business in 1835 and 1845, meeting President Jackson on the first visit. While in the capital in 1835 he posed in an army
officer's uniform for a portrait painted by Charles Bird King, repro-
duced, with a short biographical sketch, in McKenny and Hall's
Indian Tribes. In 1843 Waubansee played a leading role at an inter-
tribal conference at the Cherokee capital of Tahlequah (now in Oklahoma), which endeavored to unify the immigrant tribes and facilitate

relations with the indigenous tribes.

There is controversy about the time and manner of Waubansee's death. Twenty years after, Alexander Robinson told Lyman Draper that the chief died as a result of injuries received in a stagecoach accident while returning from Washington. Others maintain that he died of a fever in 1848, shortly before his tribe was removed to Kansas.

In Iowa his name is on Wabonsie Creek and State Park in Fremont county, and Waubonsie township in Ringgold county. In Kansas, Wabaunsee county was named for him in 1855. In Illinois his name is on Waubansee Creek, a tributary of the Fox River near Oswego, a town which has also named a park and a library for him. Also named for him is Waubonsee Community College at Sugar Grove in Kane County, the community of Wauponsee in Grundy County, and Wabansia Avenue in Chicago.

The meaning of his name is "Early Day," or literally "Little Dawn," although other explanations abound, and several reasons for the name are in print. According to Governor Reynolds and General Harrison, it was given because he boarded one of Harrison's supply boats on the Wabash in October 1811, at the break of day, and killed a man. According to Alexander Robinson in 1866, the name meant "foggy morning," and was given because the above raid, and another in which he was wounded, took place on foggy mornings. Another account places this incident on White River, while yet another says his name was acquired because he scalped an Osage warrior inside a stockade at daybreak. Other translations of his name include "looking glass," "he lives through the winter," "causer of paleness," and "the white sky."

Sources

Hiram Beckwith, *Illinois and Indiana Indians* (New York: Arno Press, 1975, Reprint), p. 172n.

J.M. Bisbey, "Pioneering in Waubansee County," Collections *Kansas Historical Society*, Vol. 2 (1909-10), pp. 594-595.

J.N. Bourassa, "The Life of Wah-bahn-se: The Warrior Chief of the Potawatamies," *Kansas Historical Quarterly*, Vol. 38, No. 2 (Summer, 1972), pp. 132-43.

James A. Clifton, *Prairie People, Continuity and Change in Potawatomi Indian Culture, 1665-1965* (Lawrence: The Regents Press of Kansas, 1977).

Seth Dean, "Wabaunsee, The Indian Chief (A Fragment)," *Annals of Iowa*, 3d series, Vol. 16, No. 1 (July 1927), pp. 3-24.

Draper Notebooks, S-21, p. 280, State Historical Society of Wisconsin.

R. David Edmunds, *The Potawatomis: Keepers of the Fire* (Norman: University of Oklahoma Press, 1978).

Mrs. John Kinzie, *Wau-Bun* (Chicago: Rand McNally Co., 1901), pp. 134, 187.

S. MacCarty to Lyman Draper, December 20, 1881, Tecumseh MSS, Vol. 9, December, 1869, State Historical Society of Wisconsin.

Thomas L. McKenney and James Hall, *History of the Indian Tribes*, 3 Vols. (Philadelphia, 1855), Vol. 3, pp. 31-35.

Charles Kappler, *Indian Treaties* (New York: Interland Publishing Co., 1972), pp. 133, 276, 296, 298- 99, 353-54, 404, 415.

Henry R. Schoolcraft, *Historical and Statistical Information Respecting the History, Conditions, and Prospects of the Indian Tribes of the United States*, 6 Vols. (Philadelphia: Lippincott Grambo Co., 1851-56), Vol. 5, pp. 530-531.

J.A. Swisher, "Chief Waubonsie," *The Palimpsest*, Vol. 29, No. 12 (December 1948), pp. 353-361.

Virgil J. Vogel, *Indian Place Names in Illinois* (Springfield: Illinois State Historical Society, 1962), pp. 160-62.

_____, *Iowa Place Names of Indian Origin* (Iowa City: University of Iowa Press, 1983), pp. 100-102.

Watseka
Potawatomi
ca. 1810 - 1878

The Potawatomi Indians had a tradition that the Iroquois once attacked one of their villages in Illinois, on the banks of a stream that has been called the Iroquois River ever since. From the river the county was named, and for the Potawatomi heroine of that engagement, Watch-e-kee or Watseka, the county seat ultimately was named.

According to the story, the Iroquois drove off the Potawatomi with great slaughter. When the refugees gathered at night some distance away, a courageous woman exhorted the men to counter-attack, since the victors were celebrating and would not expect danger. When the warriors hesitated, the woman said she would organize the women to fight, since they might as well die fighting as be killed next day by the Iroquois. When the women responded in large numbers, the men were shamed into marching against the Iroquois, whom they surprised and routed. A council of the tribe then decreed that whenever the heroic woman died, her name, Watch-e-kee, would be bestowed on the most accomplished maiden of the tribe, and handed down from one generation to the next.

While that story cannot be documented, there was in fact a Potawatomi woman called Watch-e-kee, who was born along the Kankakee River in Illinois about 1810. She was a niece of Tamin, a local chief, and at a tender age was given in marriage to Gordon S. Hubbard, a trader for the American Fur Company on the Iroquois River, who was destined to become a leading citizen of Chicago. Such unions were often arranged for business or convenience, and when the fur trade declined, Hubbard, after a two-year union resulting in a daughter who did not survive, abandoned the "Pretty Woman" (one translation of her name), and moved to Chicago in 1829. The deserted girl later married a Frenchman named Noel le Vasseur, and lived for a time at Bourbonnais on the Kankakee. After mothering several children, she left le Vasseur in 1837 to join her tribe which had, by terms of the Chicago treaty of September 25, 1833, migrated to a reservation near the site of present Council Bluffs, Iowa, in 1835. There she married another Frenchman named Bergeron. According to one report she died in 1842, but more romantic accounts claim that she returned to Illinois in 1863 to view the scenes of her youth. The story might be true, for in the same year residents of South Middleport, a village at the junction of Sugar Creek and Iroquois River, decided to rename their settlement in her honor, adapting her name to the euphonious form of Watseka. On her last visit she is portrayed as a forlorn woman, typifying the fading destiny which writers of that day assigned to her people. One account reads:

> She plodded her weary way afoot and alone to the scenes of her childhood and visited the graves of her kindred and tribe. ... Sadly she left, as the last Potawatomie to set foot on the soil of Iroquois county, and returned to Kansas [where the Potawatomi then lived] and about the year 1878, in the Potawatomie reservation in Kansas, passed to the "happy hunting grounds."

Sources

Hiram Beckwith, *History of Iroquois County* (Chicago: H.H. Hill Co., 1882), Part 2, p. 25.

Milo M. Quaife, *Chicago's Highways Old and New* (Chicago: D.F. Keller Co., 1923, reprint, Ann Arbor: University Microfilms, 1968), pp. 63-65.

Virgil J. Vogel, *Indian Place Names in Illinois* (Springfield: Illinois State Historical Society, 1962), pp. 159-160.

Salem Ely, *A Centennial History of the Villages of Iroquois and Montgomery and the Township of Concord* (Chicago: Regan Printing House, 1918), pp. 13-14. For a variation of the Watseka legend, see Alanson Skinner, *The Mascoutens or Prairie Potawatomi Indians* (Milwaukee: Milwaukee Public Museum, 1927), Part III, pp. 393-395. In this version, the invading tribe is the Kiowa, and the heroine is Watasa-kao, "Brave Woman."

Carlos Montezuma

Christine Migwans

Carlos Montezuma (1866?-1923), an early crusader for Native American rights, was born at a time when "...the Anglo-American world was rapidly enclosing the world of the Indians of Arizona" (Iverson, 4). Montezuma was an Arizona Yavapai called Wassaja (meaning "signaling" or "beckoning") by his parents. He was captured by Pimas as a young boy and sold to a childless Italian immigrant named Carlos Gentile, a photographer who had visited the reservation.

Gentile cared for young Carlos, who attended schools in Chicago and Galesburg, Illinois, and Brooklyn, New York, from 1872 until 1878. Then Montezuma moved to Urbana, Illinois, to live with a Baptist minister's family until he began college. Montezuma earned a B.S. in Chemistry from the University of Illinois, and then attended the Chicago Medical College, earning an M.D. in 1889.

Until 1896, Montezuma worked for the Federal Indian Bureau (which became the Bureau of Indian Affairs in 1947) as a physician at various Indian Bureau boarding schools. The last of these was Carlisle Indian school, in Pennsylvania, where he served from 1893 until 1896. The director of Carlisle was Richard H. Pratt, to whom Montezuma took an instant liking, and with whom he remained close friends throughout his adult life. Pratt, like Montezuma, believed Indians needed to assimilate into white society or remain forever oppressed. Montezuma's efforts as a crusader for Indian rights thus began in his experiences at Carlisle.

When Montezuma left Carlisle in 1896 he moved to Chicago and opened an office, working as a physician on his own. Although successful in his own career, Montezuma despaired at the lack of improvement in the Native American condition. He spoke out against the Indian Bureau's system of controlling Indian lives. Arguing that reservations trapped and demoralized Indians, he believed Indians had to get away from reservations. He advanced his argument through speeches, lectures, and articles he wrote for newspapers and various journals.

In 1901 Carlos Montezuma decided to return to the places of his boyhood. Later, he best remembered his visit to Adamsville. The first person he met there was an old man who could not speak English. Through an interpreter, Montezuma found out the old man had lived in the area for forty years. Montezuma decided to ask him if he recalled a photographer from thirty-one years ago who had purchased a young boy. The old man's response was "yes." Montezuma pointed to himself and said, "I am that Indian boy" (p. 42). Quickly hands extended to bid welcome to a lost son of the tribe. So began his relationship with his homeland and tribe, a relationship which lasted the rest of his life.

Carlos Montezuma emerged as a national leader for Native Americans between 1905 and 1911. He played a strong role in the development of the Society of American Indians (SAI), a group composed of American Indians from across the United States, and in the affairs of the Fort McDowell reservation in Arizona.

The SAI held its first annual meeting in 1911. The SAI consisted of individuals with significant education and experience in white America. Although white scholars and officials helped found the SAI, it soon became an all-Indian organization. The well-educated Native Americans who comprised SAI membership believed in a bright Indian future and they contributed significantly to the prospect, both within the organization and in their own personal lives.

Carlos Montezuma actively supported the SAI. He was a regular contributing writer and editor to its quarterly publication. He sometimes believed the organization did not demand enough from the federal government, however. It was Montezuma's contention that the abolition of the Federal Indian Bureau would be the best first step toward the solution of many of the problems facing Indians. So in 1916, he founded the newsletter to which he gave his own name, *Wassaja*. In *Wassaja*, Montezuma publicly protested the Indian Bureau but supported the SAI and the Fort McDowell reservation, his homeland. He believed that Indian people would grow in numbers and not become a vanishing race. He also used *Wassaja* as a forum to analyze the role of other institutions (schools and churches, for instance) in Indian affairs.

Montezuma became heavily involved in the battle for water rights of the Yavapai in southern Arizona. He fought to save the homeland of his people. He encouraged his people to remain on their lands and not be removed to a nearby Pima reservation. His battle became an outright challenge to the Indian Bureau.

Montezuma spent the last three years of his life attempting to become an enrolled member of the San Carlos Reservation. This was the only time when the Indian Bureau was able to extract a little revenge, by denying his countless attempts to become an enrolled member. Montezuma did have, however, the satisfaction of coming home.

He continued his journal while slowly dying of tuberculosis. As a physician he knew he was not going to get better. In his last issue of *Wassaja* in November, 1922, he spoke of the remaining struggle for the Society of American Indians:

> "... if the world be against us, let us not be dismayed, let us not be
> discouraged, let us look up and go ahead, and fight on for freedom
> and citizenship of our people. If it means death, let us die on the
> pathway that leads to the emancipation of our race; keeping in
> our hearts that our children will pass over our graves to victory."
> (p. 173)

Carlos Montezuma was an extraordinary man. He has earned a
valuable place in Indian history. Through his writings and his
speeches, he helped lead the fight for Indian rights at a time when
the United States government was denying those rights in various
ways. Montezuma knew Indians would endure. Carlos Montezuma
was buried in his homeland on the Fort McDowell reservation in Arizona in 1923.

Source

Peter Iverson, *Carlos Montezuma and the Changing World of American Indians* (Albuquerque: University of New Mexico Press, 1982).

4. LAND

Land and Lifeway in the Chicago Area: Chicago and the Illinois-Miami

Jay Miller

Chicago has long been something of a cosmopolitan community because it includes the location of a useful, if minor, portage between Lake Michigan and the Illinois river, leading ultimately to the Mississippi and the Gulf (Tanner 1987, p. 40).

Because of this, it seems likely that the Chicago area was frequented by the Illinois Indians in late prehistory and Chicago also appears as the name of several Illinois chiefs, one of whom, a Michigamea, visited France in 1725 (Temple 1966, pp. 12, 35, 41, 47). Eventually, however, European settlement, gun-toting Iroquois, hostile Sioux, and raids by Fox or Winnebago made things dangerous. During recent centuries, Chicago was a gathering place for displaced Miami and Potawatomi, among others. About 1700, "the Miami were located in several villages from the Mississippi to the St. Joseph rivers with Chicago being the center of the Miami country" (Temple 1966, p. 60).

The Midwest and western Great Lakes were homeland for tribes of the Central Algonkian, which together with Plains and Eastern divisions, comprise this stock. While the Eastern Algonkian languages are related to a common parent language (Proto-Eastern Algonkian [PEA]) that left the homeland, those of the Plains and Central Tribes are not. Each seems to be a seperate splinter group from the Proto-Algonkian homeland (about 2,000 years ago) between Georgian Bay and Lake Ontario. The modern Plains Algonkians are Blackfoot, Cheyenne and Arapaho, and the Central ones are Ojibwa, Ottawa, Cree, Potawatomi, Menominee, Fox-Sauk, Kickapoo-Mascouten, Shawnee, and Illinois-Miami. Of these, Menominee is most distinctive, while Potawatomi indicates an early closeness with Ojibwa and later contacts with Fox(Mesquaki)-Sauk-Kickapoo. Also, Ojibwa and Cree show mutual linguistic borrowing and other interchanges over a long time.

The lifeway of the Central Algonkians represents that of the Woodlands, with tribal differences often conforming to local ecological conditions and the time-depth of their adaptation to that region. Thus, while all used domed wigwams, their coverings were variously mats, bark, or skin, depending on local supplies.

After a period of sifting out, the term Illinois was applied to 5 component tribes. These were the Cahokia, Kaskaskia, Tamaroa, Michigamea, who may have had a distinct linguistic ancestry, joined the

Kaskaskia along the northern Illinois river, while the Cahokia blended with the Peoria near the confluence of the Illinois and Mississippi.

The term Miami was applied to 3 tribes, the Miami, Piankashaw and the Wea. In 1854, the last two joined with the Peorias a consequence of a consolidation movement in eastern Kansas led by Baptist Peoria (Lanapeshaw) (Anson 1970, pp. 237, 248). Their modern-day descendants are known only as the Confederated Peorias and have a tribal headquarters in northeastern Oklahoma.

Like other Woodland tribes, the Illinois-Miami practiced a skillful blend of hunting, gathering, and farming. They moved with the seasons between villages near their fields and camps in resource areas. Villages were located along streams and rivers, such as the Des Plaines, in proximity to fresh water, firewood, and level terrain, which is all too typical of the Midwest. Some of these villages were huge, with hundreds of lodges, but camps were usually quite small.

Incidentally, Chicago was such a camping place because, while native people came here to use local resources, they had better sense than to subject themselves to local wind, cold and marshes. Then as now, life was easier in the suburbs. The native term from which Chicago takes its name refers to a stink, which over time has been attributed to wild onion-like tubers gathered in the area or to a preponderance of skunks. Indeed, the name of Chicago is very close to the reconstructed Proto-Algonkian word for skunk [sheka:kwa] (Aubin 1975, pp. 141; 1978; 1979). It is this association with skunks, moreover, that has been the basis for most of the Indian stories of how Chicago got its name. Here are examples from the Menominee and the Delaware, both speakers of Algonkian languages related to those of the Illinois and the Miami.

Potawatomi living in the Chicago marshes told Menominee of the good hunting there, but when the Menominee came to visit, all they found were skunks.

Menominee also heard of an Ottawa couple who came to trap beaver on a lake between Chicago and Milwaukee. They quarrelled and the wife left, walking south and changing into a skunk who went to live "in a marsh, where Chicago now stands" (Hoffman 1896, p. 238). The hunter found many skunks there, but never learned which of them was his wife.

The Anadarko Delaware come closer to the historical record with their story of how Chicago got its name. They say there was a trader who lived where Chicago is now (which is true). and that he entertained the Indians who came to his store by doing funny things (which is not reported in the records). What the trader was best known for, however, was flatus. Old Indian ladies were particularly amused by his displays and told each other about the "old skunk" at the trading post, and that, I was told, was how Chicago was named.

As these stories indicate, Chicago was not a very important place. There were no great resources or leaders nearby. These were in the towns.

As in other tribes, the more permanent farming villages were probably led by civil or war leaders, whose authority fluctuated with social affairs. During quiet times, the chief led, but, at the declaration of war, he deferred to the leadership of the captain. Each official also would have had a staff of advisors, heralds, and aides, probably holding hereditary positions. In practice, these offices were the responsibility of elite families, all of whose members took leadership roles, whether they were male or female. This explains the mention of women chiefs and captains among the Illinois-Miami. Early records also report berdaches or transvestites for these tribes. As now understood, these were boys who took on the role of a third gender in response to a vision.

After the crops were planted and up, the able-bodied left to hunt bison. During good years, they returned in July to harvest a first crop of maize (corn). The Miami had a soft white maize different from the flint variety of surrounding tribes (Anson 1970, p. 20). A second harvest might come in late August. If game were abundant, there might be communal hunts for bison or deer in the Spring and Fall. During the Fall, people moved to camps for hunting and gathering nuts, fruits, berries, and other products. Other camps were occupied by smaller family groups during the winter to keep feeding, sheltering, and socializing manageable.

Crops consisted of maize, beans, squash, and tobacco. The Midwest also planted the earlier crops domesticated during the Archaic, such as sunflowers and tubers. Later, they acquired melons and other fruits from the French.

In addition to longhouses and camp houses, small huts were used by women during birthing or menstruation. An Illinois first entered the social world in one of these birth huts and stayed there with his or her mother during her seclusion. Afterwards, they joined their family in a longhouse. Eventually a baby was named, accepted by the clan and community, undertook a vision quest and fast at about puberty, became initiated into adult associations, married, raised a family, served as a respected elder, and died. The grieving spouse and kin kept memory of the deceased alive with feasts and festivals. At the first kill for a boy or first menstruation for a girl, special attention was given to them at a public ceremony. The girl learned to enter a menstrual hut every month thereafter until she reached menopause. Traditionally, a man or woman had to prove their economic and domestic skills, so marriage was postponed until maturity in the thirties. During historic times, however, Illinois married as late teenagers. Among the elite, a man married several wives, often sisters or kinswomen to each other, and relied on their added contributions for enhancing reputation, hospitality, and generosity of their household.

While far from clear, it seems probable that the Illinois-Miami traced descent through males, recognizing patrilineages, clans named for animals and divided into moieties (halves) linked to Earth or Sky. Animal names suggestive of clans among the Illinois include the crane, bear, white hind, turtle, and duck. Those for the Miami were wolf, loon, eagle, buzzard, cougar, turkey, raccoon, snow, sun, water, elk, bear, and crane.

Further confusing the issue is the possibility that there were tribal totems, like the game totems of Maritime Algonkians. This may be the source for the Miami name, which seems to relate to the sandhill crane. The head and neck of such a crane was long used as an emblem by the Miami, although at the 1793 Ohio conference, they signed with a turtle (Hodge 1907, p. 854).

In general, social divisions followed natural ones. Major groups corresponded to drainage patterns, with linked villages forming bands occupying the same stream. Major villages were located at the confluences of tributaries and trunk, with the overall community known by the name of this river, as in the case of the Illinois.

Lineages were probably localized along waterways, with their bond to the terrain symbolized by a bundle encasing objects holding power from one of the important local immortals. Lineages celebrated their identities at bundle rituals, often in the spring when the world awoke anew and power contacts were revived. Lineages also probably controlled a pool of names expressive of their eponym and locale.

Throughout the Woodland, the universe was believed to consist of a sphere with the earth plane at its middle. There were levels above and below the earth, often 4 in each. Overall, there was God, called Master of Life and probably equated with the Sun in ancient belief. Sometimes, there was a tube or pillar perpendicular to the earth, uniting upper and lower strata. Visions permitted individual humans to access other beings resident in the cosmos. Generally, the kinder beings lived above the earth, and the more dangerous ones lived below it. Not surprisingly, these were given more ritual attention because people were more concerned with possible harm from them.

Access to the immortals who controlled the universe was confirmed by medicine bundles (power packs) assembled by each visionary to reflect the nature of his or her vision. Particularly successful bundles might be transferred to communal ownership by a lineage, clan, village, or cult. In addition to such personal and communal bundles, men might also have warrior bundles assembled around bird skins wrapped in colorful reed matting. Among these were stone falcons, crows, turtle doves, ducks, swallows, martins, and parrots (Brown 1979, p. 243). Predatory birds, such as the falcon, had been associated with the cult of warriors since Mississippian times.

Particular rituals reported by early Europeans were the Calumet Dance, Midewiwin, and treatments by shamans. The calumet was a highly decorated pipestem with a fan of feathers, variously colored for welcome (white) or war (red). It was used as an instrument for safe conduct, display, and community well being. It was featured during arrival, gathering, and adoption ceremonies, and always treated with great reverence.

The midewiwin, also known as the Shaman's Academy, emerged about 1700 among Ojibwa settled at La Pointe, Wisconsin. Among the Woodlands, it generally consisted of nine grades: four of the Earth, four of the sky, and one for ghosts of dead members. Each grade was marked by using a pouch made from the skin of an animal species appropriate to that natural locale, mammals for earth grades and birdskins for sky ones.

So little is known about Illinois shamans that the description (as translated by Dr. Denys Delage) under "Jouglerie," written in intermingled Peoria and French, in the dictionary of Jean Le Boullenger bears special attention. Costume details include moccasins with fur on the outside, deer-like legs, a complete bear skin worn as a cloak, hooked finger and toe nails, and what may have been a mask with bent horns, snakes for hair, a long beak, and a huge, red-rimmed maw. There is a suggestion that such a shaman accompanied a newborn when it was taken from seclusion a few days after birth and presented to the sun at dawn to receive its first name.

In addition, there were ceremonies held to celebrate the bounty of nature as wild crops matured and fields became ready for harvest. Fall harvest festivals, at a time of economic overlap between the contributions of men (game) and women (crops), were particularly important.

Such rituals reinforced the cohesion of the Illinois and the Miami, but that cohesion suffered greatly during the long period of hostilities. The labors of French priests also did much to erode community solidarity. Important features of the process by which the Illinois became displaced and dispersed have been discussed by Brown (1979), although the more recent history of the Confederated Peoria has not been reported.

The Miami have maintained a more integrated identity into the present. When Indiana became a state its wealthiest inhabitants were Miami leaders, Francois Godfroy and Jean-Baptiste

Richardville, who "reputedly became the richest man in Indiana before his death in 1841" (Rafert 1982, p. 10).

Sources

Bert Anson, *The Miami Indians* (University of Oklahoma Press, 1970), 329 pp.

George Aubin, *A Proto-Algonquian Dictionary* (National Museum of Man, Mercury Series 29, 1975), 191 pp.

Natalia Belting, "Illinois Names for Themselves and Other Groups," *Ethnohistory*, Vol. 5, No. 3 (1958), pp. 285-291.

Margaret Kimball Brown, *Cultural Transformations Among The Illinois: An Application Of A Systems Model*, Michigan State University Museum, Anthropology Series Vol. 1, No. 3 (1979), pp. 217-267.

Frederick Hodge, ed. *Handbook of American Indians North of Mexico*, Bureau Of American Ethnology, Bulletin 30 (1907).

W.J. Hoffman, *The Midewiwin or "Grand Medicine Lodge" Of The Ojibwa*, BAE-AR 7 (1891), pp. 143-300.

W.J. Hoffman, W.J. "The Menomimi," in *Annual Report of the Bureau of American Ethnology*, Vol. 14 (1896), 328 pp.

W. Vernon Kinietz, "Miami," in *The Indians of the Great Lakes 1615-1760* (University of Michigan Press: Ann Arbor Paperbacks, 1940), pp. 161-225.

Ruth Landes, *Ojibwa Religion and the Midewiwin* (University of Wisconsin Press, 1968), 250 pp.

Jean La Boullenger, *French-Illinois Dictionary* [1718], original in the John Carter Brown Library, Providence, Rhode Island.

Stewart Rafert, *The Hidden Community: The Miami Indians of Indiana, 1846-1940* (Ph.D. dissertation, University of Delaware, 1982).

Helen Hornbeck Tanner, *Atlas of Great Lakes Indian History* (Norman: University of Oklahoma Press, 1987), 224 pp.

Wayne Temple, *Indian Villages of the Illinois Country. Historic Tribes*, Illinois State Museum Scientific Papers, Vol. 2, part 2, 218 pp.

Bruce Trigger, "Northeast," in *Handbook of North American Indians*, Vol. 15 (Washington, D.C.: Smithsonian), 924 pp.

C.C. Trowbridge, *Meearmeear Traditions*, Vernon Kinietz, ed. (University of Michigan Museum Of Anthropology, Occasional Contributions 7, 1938), 91 pp.

Treaties and Land Cessions

Dorene Wiese
Christine Red Cloud
Margaret Red Cloud
Terry Straus
Lincus Harris

Treaties are agreements negotiated between sovereigns. The United States negotiated some 372 different treaties with Indian nations, many of which were problematic in familiar ways: "tribes" were established and "chiefs" appointed by the US for the purpose of negotiations; and texts were written in English which few Indian people could read or understand and interpreters misrepresented their content, yet federal officials were bound only by what was written, not what was said; alcohol was liberally used to encourage Indian compliance; and, ultimately, abrogations became acceptable as an attribute of the federal trust relationship.

In 1871, during the federal campaign to confine western Indians, Congress unilaterally declared an end to treaty-making with Indian tribes, on the grounds that they could not rightfully be considered nations. Thereafter, negotiated settlements between the US and Indian tribes were called "agreements." Treaties and agreements both concerned land cessions on the part of Indian groups in exchange for certain goods and services on the part of the federal government. The Indian people did not conceive of land as property to be owned: they agreed to share occupancy and use of their homelands with the immigrants. Those agreements, however, established the dispossession and removal of their people. Today, they abide by those treaties and agreements and expect the federal government to do so as well.

INDIAN TREATIES AFFECTING CHICAGO

There have been five treaties of particular interest to Chicago, signed respectively in 1795, 1816, 1821, 1829, and 1833.

Treaty of 1795

After the death of Pontiac in 1769 the Potawatomi joined the Miami and others under the leadership of Little Turtle, chief of the Miami, in their resistance to Generals Harmar, St. Clair and Wayne in 1790, 1791 and 1793-9. After General Anthony Wayne had administered an overwhelming defeat to the Indians in the battle of Fallen Timbers in 1794, the Potawatomi took part in the signing of the Treaty of Greenville on August 3, 1795. This treaty was signed by Little Turtle and by General Wayne. A vast tract of land was ceded to the government by the terms of this treaty. Along with other items in the treaty was the cession of a "piece of land six miles square at the mouth of the Chikago river, emptying into the southwest end of Lake Michigan." This a few years later became the site of Fort Dearborn.

Treaty of 1816

In 1816, at St. Louis, the Potawatomi ceded a long strip of land southwestward from Lake Michigan to the Illinois and Fox rivers, twenty miles in width. The northern boundary of this strip was ten miles north of the Chicago river, and was long known as "The Indian Boundary Line." The street marking this boundary line in Chicago is now known as Rogers Avenue; Indian Boundary Park contains a plaque commemorating the 1816 treaty.

The purpose of this treaty was to secure land for a canal from Lake Michigan to the Illinois river and for a military road to aid in its building. Twenty years later the digging of this canal—the Illinois and Michigan canal—was started, though the canal was not completed until 1848.

Indians of the Chicago Region
Treaty of 1821

The Chicago treaty of 1821 gave the Americans five million acres of land on the eastern side of Lake Michigan. Chief Metea, the historian and orator of the Potawatomi, made a speech on this occasion that ranks high among Indian speeches and even among those of the [more cultured] white man. He said, in part, addressing Governor Lewis Cass of the Michigan Territory:

> "My Father, a long time has passed since we first came upon our lands; and our old people have all sunk into their graves. They had sense. We are all young and foolish, and do not wish to do anything they would not approve, were they living. We are fearful we shall offend their spirits if we sell our lands; and we are fearful we shall offend you if we don't sell them. This has caused us great perplexity of thought, because we have counseled among ourselves, and we do not know how we can part with our land. My

Father, our country was given to us by the Great Spirit, who gave it to us to hunt upon, and to make our beds upon when we die. And he would never forgive us, should we bargain it away. When you first spoke to us for land at St. Mary's, we said we had a little, and agreed to sell you a piece of it, but we could spare no more. Now you ask us again. You are never satisfied.

"My Father, we have sold you a great tract of land already, but it is not enough. We sold it to you for the benefit of your children, to farm and to live upon. You are gradually taking away our hunting ground. Your children are driving us before them. We are growing uneasy. What lands you have, you may retain forever, but we shall sell no more.

"My Father, we have now told you what we had to say. It was determined in council among ourselves, and what I have spoken is the voice of a friend."

It was an eloquent speech, but in spite of its sentiments the treaty was signed, and the government received the land on payments of money. Among the grants of land in this treaty were two to children of Jean B. Beaubien; each received a half section of land on the Washtenaw river.

Treaty of 1829

In 1827 the Winnebagos of Wisconsin went on the warpath and urged the Potawatomi to join them. The inhabitants of the little settlement at Fort Dearborn greatly feared attack by their Potawatomi neighbors. Sauganash, Shabbona and Robinson, however, persuaded the Potawatomi not to join the Winnebagos, and forestalled an attack.

In 1829, at Prairie du Chien in Wisconsin, near the junction of the Mississippi and Wisconsin rivers, the Potawatomi signed the fourth of the treaties that affected Chicago. In accordance with the terms of this treaty, the government received the lake front from Rogers Avenue, the former Indian Boundary Road, north to Kenilworth. This cession embraced Evanston and Wilmette and lands to the west.

The 1829 treaty included several important grants to individual Indians. Archange, Indian wife of Antoine Ouilmette, received for herself and her children two sections of land on Lake Michigan south of and adjoining the north boundary of the land ceded to the government. Sauganash received two and a half sections above and adjoining the line of the purchase of 1816, known as the Indian Boundary Line. Chechepinqua also was granted two sections on the Des Plaines river. None of these lands is presently in Indian hands, but local place names reflect the history of ownership.

Treaty of 1833

In the fall of 1833 thousands of Indians gathered in Chicago at the request of Governor Lewis Cass to consider the cession of the last of their lands east of the Mississippi. Most of these Indians were Potawatomi.

By 1833, the Potawatomi had already negotiated 24 treaties with the US. They had seen the inevitable expansion of American claims. Black Hawk's group of Sauk, Fox, and Kickapoo had just been defeated in their efforts to reclaim lands ceded in 1804 by representatives who were drunk and who had no authority to represent the tribes. Black Hawk's group sought to reoccupy their homelands rather than submit to removal. Removal appeared inevitable. The Potawatomi in the area knew they would be forced to relinquish their lands and to move: what they could negotiate were the conditions of that cession and removal.

There were many who were given special grants in this treaty. Among them were Sauganash, Shabbona, Chechepinqua, Antoine Ouilmette, Medore and Charles Beaubien, Joseph Bailly and James Kinzie. Sixty years after the signing of this treaty Chief Simon Pokagon was still trying to collect the money due the tribe from the government, to the amount of $180,000, without interest. This was not fully paid until 1896.

Although historians commonly represent the fact that the Potawatomi were pushed out of Illinois, the Potawatomi are still here in Illinois, and have been here for well over two hundred years. Intertribal marriage was one of the ways the Potawatomi remained in this area, and then later on through the government's Relocation Act. Many of the Potawatomi clan names have disappeared, through intermarriages of non-Indian and Indian, and also because of the Jesuits' random changing of clan names to biblical names. Because of the changed names, it is difficult to point out Potawatomi families in Chicago, and many people may not be aware of the fact that they are Potawatomi. Many families through intertribal marriages generation after generation, include a mixture of tribes. Individuals usually end up claiming the more familiar or recognizable tribe. Today a few recognizable Potawatomi names are evident in Chicago, names such as Wesaw and Thunder (who are part of the Potawatomi who settled in Zoar, a little community just outside of Neopit, Wisconsin), and Shegonee (who are part of the Potawatomi of Mayetta, Kansas).

However, in 1833, "All those who had worked to make Chicago an American place, rather that a Potawatomi or a French or an English district, were ... rewarded. ... If there was any larger symbol in the 1833 Chicago treaty it was that it marked the end of an era—the passing of the Indian frontier" (Clifton 1980, p. 95).

Source

James A. Clifton, "Chicago, Sept 14, 1833: The Last Great Indian Treaty in the Old Northwest," in *Journal of Chicago Historical Society*, Summer 1980, pp. 86-97.

Land Cessions: Map

Helen Tanner

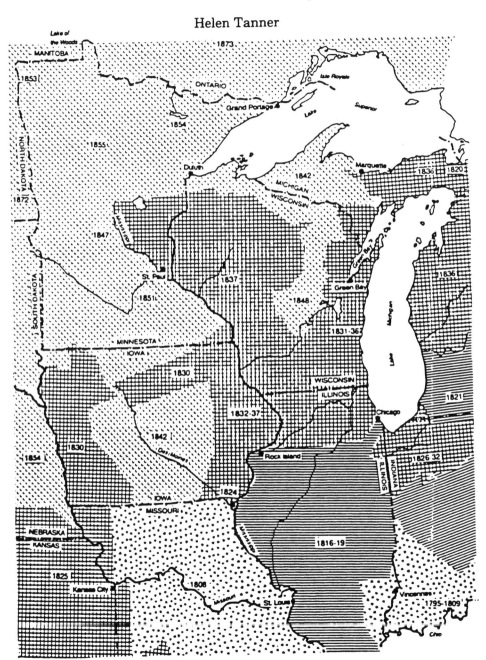

Land Cessions in the Great Lakes Area, 1783-1873:
Map 30 adapted from Tanner, Helen Hornbeck: *Atlas of Great Lakes Indian History* (198-) with permission from the University of Oklahoma Press (Norman & London).

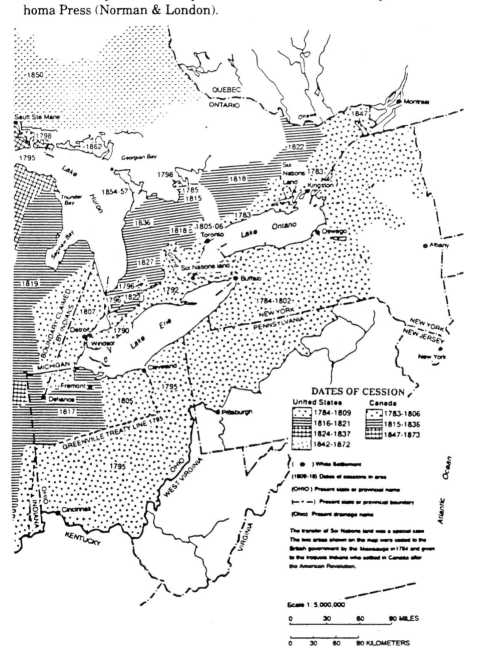

5. INDIAN HISTORY IN CONTEMPORARY CHICAGO

The Fur Trade in the Chicago Area
Yvonne Murry

Indian Villages and Trails in the Chicago Area
Vince Catches, Terry Straus, Debra Anderson

Chicago Monuments to American Indians
Nora Lloyd

The Fur Trade in the Chicago Area

Yvonne Murry

The purpose of this paper is to give a brief history of the development of the fur trade in the Chicago area. The fur trade endeavors of first the French, then British, and finally the American fur trade companies and its effects on the surrounding Indian tribes will be the specific focus.

Prior to the European invasion there were at least twenty-one major Indian villages in the Chicago area, all located on waterways. The Chicago river and its branches, the Des Plaines, the Du Page, the Calumet and the lake shore were inhabited by the Illinois tribes.

In 1673, trader Louis Joliet set forth from St. Larace on an expedition to the lower Mississippi river, during which his companion, Pere Jacques Marquette established a mission among the Illinois tribes. The establishment of Fort St. Louis on the Illinois river in 1682 with a trading post and mission was a factor in assembling a temporary local population of eighteen thousand Illinois, Miami and Shawnee. In 1680, the Iroquois attacked the Illinois tribes, chasing them along the Illinois river. In 1682 the Illinois returned with the establishment of Fort St. Louis at Starved Rock near Utica, Illinois. The purpose of Fort St. Louis and other French forts set up in the 1680s and 1690s was to protect their allies to the West, particularly from further Iroquois attacks. The Iroquois attacked Fort St. Louis unsuccessfully in 1684 and, in 1687, slaughtered members of the Miami in an area south of Fort Chicago, which was established ca. 1682. In 1696, the French began to withdraw from the fur trade efforts in the Great Lakes area for a number of reasons; no demand for the furs in Europe, depleted funds, and Jesuit complaints regarding the atmosphere of immorality in the French forts. This brought hardship to Great Lakes Indian tribes particularly to the Illinois tribes. Between 1700 and 1763, the number of Illinois Indians dwindled from 6,000 to 2,000. Alcoholism, disease and attacks from anti-French tribes were factors in the Illinois tribes decline in numbers (Tanner 1987, p. 42).

In the middle of the seventeenth century, the Neutral and later the Iroquois began to attack the southern Michigan tribes in their efforts to acquire more furs for the Europeans. Thus the Miami, the Sauk, Fox, Kickapoo, Mascouten and Potawatomi retreated west to the prairie and wild rice areas of Illinois and Wisconsin where they came into contact with the Menominee and Sioux. Major cultural changes occurred among the various Indian tribes as well as creating economic and political difficulties that led all involved to become further dependent on the fur trade. Lyle M. Stone, in the *Handbook of North American Indians*, Vol. 15:

> The impact of the European presence in the Indians lives became staggering. Beaver areas determined trade routes and tribal locations, which in turn led to the eventual establishment of Jesuit missions. These missions became economic and social centers as bands and tribes traveled there on the urging of traders and missionaries. This alteration of native settlement patterns was clearly advantageous to the interdependent religious and economic interests of the French. The geographic and cultural basis for distinct tribal or band identities were being undermined as the central feature of native life become the influence of the French military, political, economic and religious interests.

To call any French mission a specific tribe's locale would be inaccurate as many groups either lived at a specific mission or frequently went there to trade. In other words, native systems of economy, religion and warfare had changed to such a degree that French interests were becoming a major determinant of Indian activities.

Although the French were once again in the licensed fur trade business in 1720, better prices and more adequate supplies of trade goods attracted the Indian hunters of the lower Great Lakes to British traders by 1742. As per Helen Tanner in her *Atlas of Great Lakes Indian History*, the British economic advantage increased further when the French began auctioning trade posts to prospective French traders who in turn passed this added expense on to their consumers by increasing the costs of French trade goods. In 1754, competition between France and Great Britain over trading territory in the Ohio valley expanded into full-scale warfare. The tide of battle finally began to favor the British in the fall of 1758. Fort Michilimackinac, the most important post in the Great Lakes area, was occupied by the British in 1761. Illinois remained French territory and was part of French Louisiana when Pontiac's war broke out in 1763. It was ceded to Great Britain on February 10, 1763, in the Treaty of Paris.

Pontiac's objective was to expel the British from the Great Lakes area. Helen Tanner states that Pontiac's reasons were threefold: 1) the British did not give out ammunition as the French had done; 2) the British showed they wished to take over the whole country rather than contenting themselves with military and trading posts; 3) the British were arrogant and did not like the Indians (Tanner p. 48). By 1764, resistance to British occupation transferred to the Illinois country. This culminated in a peace treaty in which Pontiac stated the British would occupy the French forts only and leave Indian hunting grounds alone. In 1775, the American revolution broke out and the various Indian tribes did not initially choose sides in this war. They viewed the conflict as essentially a "father and son" issue. The tribes of Illinois country who were pro-French and had developed ties to the Spanish began acting in the American interest between 1778 and 1781 (Tanner p. 92). Also during this period of time, Spanish Louisiana became a refuge for many old French families of the Illinois country and also a residential base for Indian people put off with dealing with British and American fur traders.

In 1803, Fort Dearborn was built. By this time the Miami had largely been drawn toward the Wabash valley. Migration from Michigan between 1815 and 1830 increased the number of villages and total population of the Illinois Potawatomi. This migration was due to a search for richer hunting grounds. In 1810, the transition from British to American dominance over the fur trade was evidenced by the acquisition of smaller fur trading companies operated by British subjects at Green Bay, Prairie du Chien, and Michilimackinac by an enterprising American named John Jacob Astor. There were lavishly financed ventures from New York and Montreal which resulted in a regionwide monopoly between 1811 and 1834 led by John Jacob Astor's American Fur Company. The Indian villages in Chicago were occupied by United Bands of Chippewa, Ottawa and Potawatomi. When Astor's business was no longer profitable, he sold his Great Lakes holdings and the remaining fur trade employees were left to make the difficult transition into the new world filtering in from the East. As Jacqueline Peterson (1977) notes, "No member of the fur trade, either white or native, escaped the anguish dealt by the extinction of the fur trade and the transition to a highly organized and stratified society launched by the Yankee invasion of the old Northwest." Another factor in the changing Chicago area was the building of a new road from Detroit to Chicago bringing with it large numbers of American immigrants from the east.

The year 1830 signaled the rapid decline of the fur trade east of the Mississippi. For Indian people, ceding land and receiving annuities became a new method of subsistence, for some indispensable for survival. With the loss of the fur trade occupations, the French-Indian, creole and metis populations gradually disappeared from the Chicago area. The disappearance culminated in the Treaty of 1833, when the United Potawatomi, Chippewa and Ottawa nation ceded all its land east of the Mississippi in exchange for five million acres of promised soil. During the late 1830s, the United Bands were relocated to reservations in Iowa and eastern Kansas. Certain Chicago mixed bloods of prominence were given parcels of land as reservations for themselves so to speak. An examples of this was Billy Caldwell, the son of an

Irish military man and a Mohawk mother. His parcel of land has since been incorporated into the county forest preserves, thus the present day Caldwell woods on Chicago's north side. Beaubien woods on Chicago's far south side is named for a member of the Beaubien family, a family of French Indian extraction.

Although the Chicago area was not the center of commercial activity during the fur trade era as it is today, clearly it exhibited a dynamic inter-cultural economic system and the Indians in the area were heavily impacted by contact with the Europeans involved in the Great Lakes fur trade.

Sources

Jacqueline Peterson, "Wild Chicago: The Formation and Destruction of a Multiracial Community on the Midwestern Frontier, 1816-1837," in *The Ethnic Frontier: Essays in the History of Group Survival in Chicago and the Midwest*, edited by Melvin Holli and Peter Jones (William B. Eerdmans Publishing Company, 1977).

Lyle M. Stone and Donald Chaput, "History of the Upper Great Lakes Area," in *Handbook of North American Indians*, edited by Bruce G. Trigger (Washington, D.C.: Smithsonian Institution, 1978), Vol. 15.

Helen Hornbeck Tanner, *Atlas of Great Lakes Indian History* (Norman: University of Oklahoma Press, 1987).

Indian Villages and Trails in the Chicago Area

Vince Catches, Terry Straus, Debra Anderson

Indian villages clustered along waterways in the Chicago area. There has been some archeological investigation of Chicago Native American sites, the most recent discovery being the remains of a village at Milwaukee and Irving Park roads. However, in most cases, there is little to mark or commemorate Native American villages publicly. Many village sites indicated on the following 1804 map are today shopping areas or apartment complexes such as that on North Avenue at the Des Plaines river. The village and mound site off Fullersburg between the river and the canal is the area of the present Graue Mill Forest Preserve (DuPage County), but none of the present personnel in the park is familiar with that part of the local history.

The burial mound associated with the Potawatomi village on the Des Plaines near Forest Park is an exception. That village and mound are indicated on the revised segment of the Scharf map.

The mound is located on what is now the Forest Home Cemetery. The cemetery was the homestead of Ferdinand Haase, who crossed the Des Plaines River on the first train on the Galena Division of the Northwestern in 1849. Succeeding generations of the Haase family managed the cemetery for more than a century. A large section of the land had earlier belonged to Leon Bourrassa, a halfbreed, and his Potawatomi wife native to the village in question. Bourrassa had received title some years after the Black Hawk War in which he warned settlers of the area of the Indian approach.

The burial mound remains today and is known as "Indian Hill." A seven foot granite monument marks the mound and holds the following inscription:

This is the site of a village and burial ground of the Potawatomi Indians from ancient times until 1835, when they were exiled to lands beyond the Mississippi. Later this locality was known as Indian Hill.

Here stood the cabin of Leon Bourrassa, the trapper. His Indian wife, Margaret, had been reared in this grove and, after the exodus of her tribe, she chose to remain near the graves of her ancestors.

In 1832 federal troops under Gen. Winfield Scott skirted this grove, forded the river a mile north, and marched on to the Black Hawk war in the Rock river country, These soldiers had encamped at a point that is now the village of Riverside to rest and recover from an epidemic of Asiatic cholera.

Upon the arrival of white settlers these acres became the homestead of Ferdinand Haase and his family. The first person to die in this new home was buried on this hill in 1854.

> "Thus, many years ago Ferdinand Haase and his sons reestab-
> lished and dedicated to sepulchre the ancient forest home of the
> Potawatomis to become the present Forest Home of the white
> man."
> —Arthur Woltersdorf

Artifacts from the mound, especially Canadian trade silver, have
been studied and described by James Van Stone, now of the Field
Museum. Donated by Isabel Wasson, the collection is kept at the Forest Park Library.

Also in the Forest Home Cemetery is the Indian Head Trail
Marker, erected in 1947 to mark an old trail through woods and wild
plum bushes along the river.

It is clear from the map of trails and villages below that many Chicago streets follow what were once Indian trails, though few are
known as such. Des Plaines Avenue follows an Indian Trail which
connected Indian Hill and the Indian village at North Avenue and the
Des Plaines river. Indian Road marks the south boundary of the former reservation of the Potawatomi Chief Sauganash (Billy Caldwell),
and the forest preserve Indian Road Woods was part of his grant
under the 1829 Prairie du Chien treaty.

South of the city, the road called Sauk Trail was part of the old
Sauk Trail through Detroit and into Canada.

> The great Sauk Trail is today roughly followed by US Highway 6
> between Rock Island and Joliet, Illinois, though it arches north-
> ward after reaching the Illinois River Valley—From Joliet east-
> ward to Frankfort in Will County its route is followed by the old
> Lincoln Highway, US 30, and from there to the Indiana state line
> at Dyer. The route is followed by a road which is still called Sauk
> Trail between those points. From the Indiana line it proceeds ulti-
> mately to Detroit along lines rough matched by US 12 (Vogel
> 1985, p. 39).

Most Chicago streets which do not conform to the later rectangular
grid pattern, follow old Indian trails. Examples of such streets are
Vincennes, Archer, and Elston Avenues. Rogers Avenue follows the
Indian Boundary line north of which all Indian people in the Chicago
area had to move as a result of the 1816 treaty.

(Map reprinted from Forest Park Review, November 19, 1926, with
permission of the Forest Park Review.)

Sources

Virgil Vogel, "Indian Trails and Place Names," in *Names*, Vol. 33, nos. 1-2 (1985), pp. 39-50.

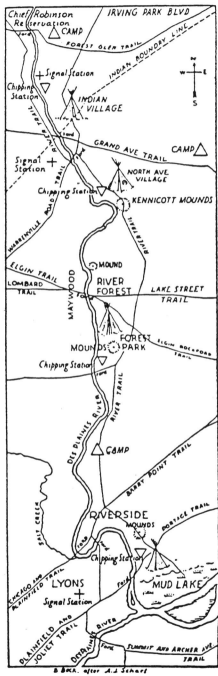

INDIAN TRAIL
Leading Through Forest Park

Chicago Landmarks

Nora Lloyd

The Marquette Building
140 South Dearborn
Chicago

Various monuments in the city of Chicago commemorate Indian people and Indian history of the city. The Marquette Building, located in the city's financial district with its constant flow of people, is perhaps the best known of such monuments. For nearly 100 years, it has represented the cooperative efforts of Indians and non-Indians in early Chicago.

The Marquette's architectural significance was immediately recognized as documented by the June 1897 issue of *Architectural Reviewer*:

> The main entrance doors are covered with plates of ornamental bronze, and the panther-heads on the push- plates of these doors were designed and executed by Edward Kerneys, the animal sculptor whose work at the World's Fair created so much favorable comment. [creator of the two lions in front of the Art Institute] Over the doors of the main entrance are panels of bronze, designed and executed by Herman A. McNeil, illustrating incidents in the life of Pere Marquette ...
>
> grand memorial rotunda, which the owners of the building, with a desire to reduce the commercial appearance and increase the artistic effect of the entrance, have devoted a large space in the center of the building to a series of decorative effects in marble, bronze, and glass mosaics of a high order. This rotunda is, I think, without a parallel in its unique treatment ...
>
> Over each elevator door on the first and second floors are portraits, in bronze, of noted Indian chiefs, together with the white men who were directly or indirectly connected with the discovery and exploration of the great Northwest...These are all modeled by Mr. Edward Kerneys, with the exception of two—Marquette and Joliet—which are by Mrs. A.A. Bradley of Boston [later confirmed to be Amy Aldis Bradley, Owen Aldis' sister] (*Architectural Reviewer*, June 1897).

The white Carrara marble in the two-story lobby set off the eleven bronze portraits which include:

First Floor

De Menthet—French Coureur-de-bois, and voyageur
Big Snake—Winnebago participant, "Thirty Years War"
Joliet—Louis Joliet, born 1645 in Quebec, explorer
Talon—Intendant of Canada under Frontenac, 1672
Noon Day—Chippewa orator prominent in Wisconsin area councils
during late 1600s
Marquette—French missionary, explorer, North America
Chicagou—Powerful Illinois chief (See Chapter 2 by Vogel, above)
Little Panther—Reputed Seneca chief
Tonti—Italian who became confidante and lieutenant to LaSalle
Shaubena—[Shabonna] An Ottawa who later became chief of Potawa-
tomis (See Chapter 2 by Vogel, above)
La Taupine—Pierre Moreau, nicknamed "La Taupine," French cour-
eur-de-bois, befriended Marquette during his last illness

Second Floor

Keokuk—The "Watchful Fox", a great orator and chief of Sac and Fox
after Black Hawk, (See Chapter 2 by Vogel, above)
Black Hawk—Sac and Fox chieftan, [Makataimeshe-kia-kiah] born in
1767, (See Chapters 2 and 3 above)
De L'Hut—Daniel Graysolen de L'Hut, cousin of Tonti and explorer
with Hennepin; city of Duluth named after him
Brown Moose—Mohawk
Chassagoac—An Illinois chief and friend of Tonti
La Salle—Rene Robert Cavalier Sieur de LaSalle, born in Rouen,
France, 1643. Educated for priesthood, traveled to Canada and
became a fur trader. Ambitious to complete explorations instituted by
Marquette, he followed Mississippi down to Gulf of Mexico
Nika—Shawnee Indian hunter who accompanied LaSalle through
Canada, Mexico and the Mississippi
War Eagle—A Potawatomi chief, participated in Black Hawk Wars
Frontenac—Governor of Canada
Hairybear—Leader of the Winnebago tribe, supporter of Marquette's
missionary work
Waubonsie—Noted war chief of the Potawatomis who befriended the
whites at Fort Dearborn (See Chapter 2 by Vogel, above)

In addition to the bronze plaques, the lobby contains some of the
most outstanding mosaic work in Chicago. A 90-foot long glass mosaic
forms the face of the balcony between the first and second floors and
vividly portrays Marquette's life with the Indians in three panels.

The panels were designed by J.A. Holzer and the materials are glass mosaics from the Tiffany Glass and Decorating Company in New York. Mr. Holzer was also the designer of much of the Chicago Public Library mosaics.

In 1978 the Marquette Building was completely restored under the direction of Walker Johnson of Holabird and Root, successor firm to the original architects, Holabird and Roche, and it has since been named a National Historic Landmark. What makes the Marquette so impressive is the successful combination of function (being one of the first commercial buildings to utilize the new structural technique, the steel frame, instead of traditional masonry wall-bearing construction) and the dedication of public space to the exhibit of top quality artwork; all in celebration of an historic time of white/Indian cooperation.

The Alarm, 1884
John J. Boyle (1851-1917)
Lincoln Park, east of Lake Shore Drive (approx. 3000N)

With its May 17, 1884 unveiling, *The Alarm* became the first monument erected on Chicago Park District property as well as the first portraying American Indians. The bronze sculpture consists of an Indian couple--the man standing next to a seated woman with papoose, his bow and quiver of arrows and dog are at his feet. Originally, four bronze bas-relief panels (now replaced with granite tablets), showed scenes of Ottawa life: "The Peace Pipe," "The Corn Dance," "Forestry," and "The Hunt."

Martin Ryerson (1818-1887) worked with the Ottawa as a young fur trader in the Chicago area and even after his financial success in the lumber business he remembered his early associations. In 1880 he commissioned "The Alarm as a memorial to "The Ottawa Nation of Indians, my early friends" (Ira J. Bach and Mary Lackritz Gray, A Guide to Chicago's Public Sculpture , The University of Chicago Press, 1983, p. 156). He was actively involved in the project to ensure that the artist "portray their strength of character and peacefulness and avoid the stereotype..." (Bach, 1983)

A Signal of Peace, 1890 (installed June 9, 1894)
Cyrus Edwin Dallin (1861-1944)
Lincoln Park, east of Lake Shore Drive, north of Diversey Harbor entrance

On horseback, a Sioux chief in full headdress is giving a traditional sign of peace near the lakeshore. Lambert Tree, a Chicago judge, saw the work at the 1893 World's Columbian Exposition and donated it to the city. Mistakenly, he explained his reasoning for the donation: "It is evident there is no future for them except as they may exist as a memory in the sculptor's bronze or stone and the painter's canvas" ("ibid ., p. 154) Judge Tree wanted a public memorial to "these simple, untutored children of nature" (idem.)

The Fort Dearborn Massacre, or *The Potawatomi Rescue*, 1893
Carl Rohl-Smith (1848-1900)
In park south of Glessner House Museum, 1800 South Prairie Avenue (Recently moved from Chicago Historical Society)

Throughout history, armed conflict has brought heavy casualties, and the War of 1812 was no exception. The Indian population in the Chicago area was not unanimous in supporting the British, and Carl Rohl-Smith chose to represent this dichotomy when he created The Fort Dearborn Massacre (The Potawatomi Rescue). The sculptor depicts Mrs. Margaret Helm (stepdaughter of fur trader John Kinzie) being saved by Potawatomi chief Black Partridge from an attacking Indian. Some reports set the battle site on property owned by railroad car manufacturer George Pullman, who commissioned the bronze memorial in 1893.

According to an article from the Evanston News-Index (c. 1941), Rohl-Smith used two Sioux Indians from the Dakotas as his models for both Potawatomis depicted in this statue. Short Bull, whom Rohl-Smith thought was "the most typical American Indian," modeled the rescuer Black Partridge; Kicking Bear was the model for the Indian attempting to scalp Mrs. Helm. Both visited Chicago as part of a Sioux delegation in 1891. The article was found at the Evanston, Illinois, Historical Society. A copy is in the Urban Records Collection of the Community Archives of NAES College.

Indians, also known as *The Bowman* and *The Spearman*, 1928
Ivan Mestrovic (1883-1962)
Entrance to Grant Park, Michigan Avenue at Congress Parkway (500 S.)

These two mounted Indian warriors, The Bowman and The Spearman, guard the Congress Parkway entrance to Grant Park. The two powerful figures were created by internationally-known artist Ivan Mestrovic and provided by the B.F. Ferguson Monument Fund to commemorate the Native American. Architects Holabird and Roche were involved in the project, with their original design locating the two figures on either side of a monumental stairway which was removed in the 1940s. "The siting of the Indians, so that they appear as silhouettes against the sky, makes them among the most dramatic monuments in Chicago" (Bach and Gray 1983, p. 19).

Marion E. Gridley, in *America's Indian Statues* (1966), suggests that Mestrovic appears to have created Plains Indians astride European draft horses.

Totem Pole, also known as *Kwanusila, The Thunderbird*,
(formerly known as *Kwa-Ma-Rolas*), Original 1929, replaced 1986, Kwakiutl Indian
Lincoln Park, east of Lake Shore Drive at Addison Avenue (3600 N.)

The custom of totem pole carving is unique to the Northwest Coast Indians, where poles were carved to commemorate important events such as births, deaths, marriages, victories. Each pole featured a family crest and included human, animal and/or mythological figures to tell the story.

The original 40-foot Lincoln Park Totem Pole was carved around the turn of the century in Alert Bay, Canada. James L. Kraft, founder of Kraft, Inc., saw the pole on a trip to the Pacific Northwest and purchased it in 1926. Kraft donated the totem pole to the Chicago Park District in 1929 as a dedication to the city's schoolchildren. Despite numerous repaintings and a fibre glass coating, fifty years of Chicago weather took their toll and in October 1985 the original pole was removed and returned to Canada. Renowned Kwakiuti artist Tony Hunt and his partner John Livingston had encouraged removal of the original pole to prevent further decay.

A replica of the pole carved by Hunt and again donated by J. L. Kraft now stands in its place. It has been treated with wood preservatives to allow it to withstand Chicago weather.

6. CHICAGO INDIANS TODAY

The Relocation Program and Urbanization
Donald Fixico

The Legal and Political Status of Indian
People in Chicago
*Sarah Gallagher, Terry Straus, Frances
Oskenaniew*

Narrative Traditions of the Chicago
American Indian Community
NAES Religion and Philosophy Class

Chicago's Native Americans: Cheechakos,
Old-Timers and Others in the City of Wild
Garlic
Virgil Vogel

Linking the Past and the Present: A
Commentary on Virgil Vogel's "Chicago's
Native Americans"
Rosalyn LaPier, David Beck

Chicago's American Indian Community
Organizations
Community Service Directory, NAES College

Chronological Index of Community
History—Chicago
David Beck

The Relocation Program
And Urbanization

Donald Fixico

The experiences of Native Americans during the war years had a two-fold effect on federal-Indian relations in the postwar period. The courageous performance of Native American men abroad and native women in the war industries at home impressed federal officials, convincing them that Indians possessed an aptitude for working side by side with other Americans. Barton Greenwood, acting commissioner of Indian affairs, estimated that 50 percent of the returning veterans had sufficient experience in working with other Americans away from the reservations to compete with them for jobs.

Unfortunately, returning Indian veterans increased the burden on the reservations' already limited economic resources. High unemployment and widespread poverty pervaded Indian country. In response, the government proposed relocating unemployed Indians or those who returned from the war to urban areas where they could find jobs. Greenwood advised that these people be moved as far as possible from their original communities to prevent them from returning easily to their homelands. Theoretically, this strategy would be conducive to successful Indian adaptation to urban living. Federal officials believed that once the new urban migrants had adjusted to living in the cities there would be no need for reservations. Until then, Indians continued to live on reservations under submarginal conditions.

The severe blizzard of 1947-48 worsened the already poor economy for Indian communities, especially for the populous Navajos in Arizona and New Mexico, who suffered extreme destitution. To help alleviate their suffering, the government supplied emergency aid, but the deplorable conditions on the reservation continued. This impelled the federal government to take one more step in establishing a job placement program, which laid the foundation for the relocation program. The Bureau of Indian Affairs began to resettle employable Indians from the Navajo Reservation in urban areas. The Interior Department soon established additional placement offices in Denver, Salt Lake City, and Los Angeles.

Relocation took its place beside termination as the second goal of federal Indian policy in the 1950s. After the withdrawal of trust restrictions from the lands, Native Americans were encouraged to pursue a livelihood in the cities. Although the program began with the Navajos, the government soon began to extend relocation services to all tribes.

In a conference with area directors in January 1951, Commissioner of Indian Affairs Dillon S. Myer had urged funding for the relocation program to begin the recruitment of Indians for urban placement. He had hoped to be able to expand the program quickly by intensifying and broadening recruitment efforts. Critics alleged that relocation had swept Indians off the reservations, scattered them throughout cities, and then they were abandoned by the Bureau. The commissioner denied that the Bureau of Indian Affairs had forced Native Americans to relocate. Myer insistently advocated relocation as a policy congruent with his philosophy of termination—the view that Native Americans should be encouraged to live without federal supervision like other Americans. Moving Indians to urban areas to work and to live would, he believed, escalate their standard of living. Although Myer enthusiastically supported relocation during his three years at the helm of the Bureau, the program failed to gain momentum during his administration.

Even though the application procedure for relocation was amazingly simple and open to young and old alike, Native Americans initially hesitated to volunteer for the new program. However, curiosity about city life eventually induced many people to apply for relocation. Native Americans of all types would frequently arrive at an agency office to inquire, "What is this relocation that I've been hearing about?" A survey of the Klamaths who were known to relocate to Chiloquin and Klamath Falls, two small urban centers near the reservation in Oregon, revealed that they were attracted to stores, schools, and movie theaters. In addition, veterans, relatives, and friends who were among the first to relocate made people on the reservation envious when they talked about their adventures and good times in the cities.

After an initial request for relocation had been filed with a BIA official at an agency or an area office, the paperwork began. After completing a review of the applicant's job skills and employment records, the official usually contacted the relocation office in the city of the applicant's choice. With clothes and personal items packed, the applicant customarily boarded a bus or train to the designated city, where he or she would be met by a relocation worker. Upon arrival, the newcomer received a check to be spent under the supervision of the relocation officer. Next, the officer usually accompanied the new urbanite to a nearby store to purchase toiletries, cookware, groceries, bedding, clothes, and an alarm clock to insure punctual arrival at work. In the city, the poorest of America's poor began a new day in what they hoped was a promising future.

Living by a strict timetable was a new experience for almost all relocated Indians. Often, instructions had to be given to show how a clock worked and the relocatee taught how to tell time. One young Crow Creek Sioux, who began to take college courses to improve his job qualifications, expressed exasperation in adjusting to an hour-by-hour schedule of classes. His traditional conviction that people should live in harmony with nature during a continuum of time conflicted with the concept of regulating one's life according to the minutes of a clock. "I nearly went crazy during the first two weeks of college," he said. "No matter where I was, I always had to be somewhere else at a certain time. There was no rest."

Relocation officers assisted the new migrants in locating places to shop for groceries, and informed them about nearby churches of their denominations. After the relocatee and his or her family were settled, the relocation worker and neighborhood clergyman visited on a regular basis. Normally, the BIA paid the relocatee's first month's rent, including clothing and groceries, and the expenses incurred while traveling to and from work. After the first month the relocatees were on their own, although Bureau workers remained available for counseling and assistance in job placement; BIA officials would keep tabs on the progress of relocatees for the next nine years.

Young adults, especially men, were the most common applicants for relocation. Frequently, they left families behind until they found jobs and housing, and then sent for their families. The most ambitious relocatees were young Indians who possessed some college education. They chose to move to large cities, far from their homelands, to escape their past poverty, and perhaps to forget their traditional heritage. Undoubtedly, they succeeded much better in the transition from native life to urbanization than less-educated relocatees. They successfully competed for jobs, and found adequate housing.

During midsummer 1951, the Bureau of Indian Affairs assigned workers to extend the relocation services in Oklahoma, New Mexico, California, Arizona, Utah, and Colorado. In November, a field office was opened in Chicago to place Navajos in jobs, but shortly afterwards, the BIA incorporated the office as a part of the relocation program to serve all Native Americans. The first relocatees arrived in Chicago in early February 1952. In all, relocation workers processed 442 Native Americans for employment in Los Angeles, Denver, and Chicago during that year. With the Bureau expanding the Navajo placement offices in Salt lake City, Denver, and Los Angeles to service all Native Americans, a new generation of urban Indians came into being.

Commissioner Dillon Myer strove to expand the services of the relocation program. For fiscal year 1952 Congress appropriated slightly more than half a million dollars for the first year's operation and authorized the opening of additional offices. In his budget request for the following year, Commissioner Dillon Myer requested 8.5 million dollars for vocational training and relocation. He recommended to Congress that the Bureau of Indian Affairs should negotiate contracts with state and private vocational schools in areas throughout the nation where employment opportunities were most available. "Unfortunately we did not get approval of this full program," said the commissioner, "although we did secure enough funds to establish a pilot relocation program throughout the country."

By the end of 1953, BIA relocation offices had placed 2,600 Indians in permanent jobs. Financial assistance during that year enabled 650 workers to move their families to the nearby communities where they worked, but Bureau officers experienced problems in locating enough jobs for relocatees. They relied primarily on public employment agencies, which too often placed relocatees in seasonal railroad and agricultural work, the lowest paying and least secure type of employment. Because of this, the program received criticism, and suggestions were made to try to find more meaningful jobs.

The Bureau of Indian Affairs' fiscal report for 1954 indicated that the relocation program had assisted 2,163 applicants. Some 1,649 persons, comprising over 400 family units and 514 single men and women, had relocated to metropolitan areas. Approximately 54 percent of the relocatees came from the three northern areas serviced by the Aberdeen, Billings, and Minneapolis offices. Forty-six percent were processed through the southern offices of Anadarko, Gallup, Muskogee, and Phoenix. Relocatees were placed in twenty different states, with Los Angeles and Chicago the leading cities in welcoming the most of the new urbanites.

To help process the increasing number of relocatees, the Bureau opened an office in Oakland in 1954; another office opened in San Francisco a year later, and in 1956 offices were established in San Jose and St. Louis. Soon, additional offices were operating in Dallas, Cleveland, Oklahoma City, and Tulsa. The rising number of applicants prompted the government to quickly expand the relocation program. By late 1954 approximately 6,200 Native Americans of an estimated 245,000 reservation population had resettled in large cities. From 1952 to 1955, in Chicago alone some 3,000 reservation Indians, mainly from the Southwest, had relocated. In fiscal year 1955, the Indian Bureau placed 3,461 Indians, including 2,656 persons from 708 family groups, and 805 single men and women. They were enrolled in thirty-three different courses of the vocational training program.

During the first week in January 1955, Commissioner Glenn Emmons addressed the Muskogee, Oklahoma, Chamber of Commerce, reaffirming the need for the relocation program. Poor land quality and the increasing Indian population required such a program in order to alleviate crowding and poverty. In a memo to the Secretary of the Interior, dated 20 May 1955, he outlined how the relocation program helped Native Americans escape poverty on the reservations: "We furnish transportation both for the worker and his family to the community he has selected. We help in finding a job, in locating a suitable home, and in getting generally adjusted in the new surroundings."

The commissioner foresaw improvement for American Indians through combining relocation and education. On 25 October, Department of the Interior officials announced the creation of a new adult education program to serve five particular tribal groups: the Seminole of Florida; the Papago of Arizona; the Rosebud Sioux of South Dakota; the Turtle Mountain Chippewa of North Dakota; and the Shoshone-Bannock of Fort Hall in Idaho, who were among the neediest of the Indian population.

Emmons recognized that a lack of educational opportunities impeded the overall advancement of Indian people. He began to stress the need to make schooling available to all Indian youngsters of normal school age, and he envisioned elementary schooling for adults who had never received any formal education. In essence, education was believed to be an important key to Indian urbanization. And educational reform soon became an integral part of the relocation program to assist Native Americans in better adjusting to and assimilating into the mainstream society.

BIA publicity portrayed relocation as a "New Deal" for Native Americans, one that offered them a chance to improve their economic status. Indian Bureau officials encouraged Indians to relocate, although ostensibly on a voluntary basis. Throughout the reservations, BIA workers circulated brochures and pamphlets suggesting that a better life awaited Indians in urban areas. Pictures of executives dressed in white shirts, wearing ties, and sitting behind business desks insinuated that similar occupational positions could be obtained by Indians. Photos of a white frame house with shutters enticed the women. The scene suggested that Indians could provide their families with similar homes in suburban America.

Unfortunately, the hard realities of urban life soon destroyed Indian hopes for a successful livelihood and dashed their many dreams. For those who left the reservation and traveled a long distance for the first time, the relocation experience was a threatening cultural shock. Once off a bus and alone in a strange, large city, relocatees encountered a foreign and threatening new world that often proved to be traumatic. Relocatees knew little about such modern gadgets as stoplights, clocks, elevators, telephones, and other everyday objects that Americans took for granted. To avoid a frightening elevator, they would climb the stairs in apartment buildings. Newly relocated Indians who had not yet mastered the English language experienced even more difficulty, and many were embarrassed to ask for assistance. A magazine article described one incident: "In situations of distress, the Indian often remains proudly silent. One relocatee was 'lost' in his room for 24 hours. He had lost the BIA address. And although he had a phone number he was 'ashamed' to ask how to dial." Perhaps the most important complaints from Indians dealt with the noise, tension, and hectic pace of the city life. Some Native American women found the outside bustle of the city too difficult to face and locked themselves in their apartments, afraid to even go to the supermarket.

Toward the end of 1955, the Muskogee area office in Oklahoma reported a decline in people volunteering for relocation from its area. Fear of big-city life inhibited many Native Americans making them feel lost, insecure, and inferior to the majority population urban white Americans. Compared to other, more aggressive urban minorities— blacks, Mexicans, and Puerto Ricans—the uneducated, traditional Indians were isolated and at the bottom of the social order.

Relocation officers attempted to prepare Indians for the drastic changes that lay ahead of them and to ease their adjustment to city life. They informed the relocatees of the conditions they would face in industrial areas—working according to a regular schedule, moving through city traffic, paying high rent, encountering hospital expenses, learning to budget money, purchasing suitable clothing for themselves and their children, and living in a generally non-Indian neighborhood. Despite these efforts, Indians going on relocation experienced considerable difficulty in adjusting to urban areas. An article in the Christian Science Monitor described the reality of an Indian couple relocating to a city. The story itself depicts a true picture of what relocations was probably like for a family.

> *Tony and Martha Big Bear and their family had just arrived in Los Angeles from the reservation. Everything was new to Martha and she never said a word and scarcely raised her eyes while holding the children during the bus ride to the relocation office. The first thing the relocation officer did was to advise Tony about spending money wisely. A $50.00 check was drawn up for Tony and he was told how to open a bank account. The Big Bears were then temporarily lodged in a nearby hotel.*
>
> *Although Tony wanted to be a commercial artist, he settled for a job in an aircraft plant. The Indian Bureau placement officer persuaded Tony to accept this job first and then he could check into the art field later after he became familiar with Los Angeles*

> *and when his family had a more permanent place to live. Every-*
> *thing was moving too fast for the Big Bears. The field office helped*
> *Tony find an apartment—a 'slum' according to most people, but it*
> *was better than anything Martha was accustomed to.*

The experience of the Big Bears could easily have been more diffi-cult. Sometimes factories closed down and welfare agencies had to assist relocated families. Out of necessity, Indian centers soon sprang up in almost every large city to help deprived Native American people by temporarily furnishing groceries and clothes. Nearly all relocatees experienced difficulties of one kind or another. A writer for the *Atlan-tic Monthly* published a true account involving Little Light, her hus-band Leonard Bear, and their five children, a family originally from a Creek Indian community in Oklahoma. "Today they are slum dwell-ers in Los Angeles, without land or home or culture or peace."

The author described meeting Little Light and her children in the chairless kitchen-dining-living room of a small shanty on the out-skirts of Los Angeles. Five children, black eyes round with wonder in their apricot faces, sheltered against her skirt. The walls were unpainted, the floor a patchwork of linoleum. Through an archway, another room was visible where three beds crowded together. A two-burner stove stood on a box, and on the only other piece of furniture in the room—a battered table—rested the remains of a dinner; some white, grease-soaked bags which had contained hamburgers and fried potatoes prepared by the restaurant a few blocks away.

In response to the interviewer's questions, Little Light spoke of how her husband went out drinking every night, of people in stores laughing at her, and about the need for a doctor for her sick child. She wanted to return to Oklahoma, but there was not enough money to go back. The woman stared solemnly, and her face became dis-torted as she lamented, "They did not tell us it would be like this."

Similar descriptions of unfortunate incidents were published in current magazines and newspapers, thereby reinforcing the negative public image of the BIA that the termination program had first cre-ated. Federal officials countered with defensive news releases:

> As some of you know—if you have been reading your magazines lately—that word "relocation" seems to upset certain people—ap-parently because it suggests uprooting the Indians from their serene pastoral environment and plunging them down in some kind of a nerve-wracking asphalt jungle. For at least a generation, and probably longer, Indian families have been moving away from the impoverished environment of reservations and seeking better opportunities.

Despite the radical socioeconomic problems facing them, the number of applicants for relocation began increasing on the whole. In the 1956 fiscal year, BIA workers processed 5,316 relocatees through four offices—Chicago, Denver, Los Angeles, and San Francisco. Of this number, 732 were single men, 373 were single women, and 424 had families. Relocation officers noted a growing interest in relocation among Indians, and a backlog of applications existed at almost all Indian agencies.

Some 12,625 reservation Indians had relocated to urban areas by 12 July 1956, and the Bureau expected another 10,000 to apply before 1 July 1957. The proliferating number of applicants prompted the BIA to enlarge the relocation. Commissioner Emmons announced in 1956 that relocation funding had more than tripled, from a level of $1,016,400 in 1955 to a current sum of $3,472,000. Increased funding enabled the Bureau to broaden its scope of relocation services. Two new offices were planned, and steps were taken to enlarge relocation guidance staffs.

The growing relocation program received encouragement from tribal councils. From July 19 to 21 Indian leaders held a conference in Omaha, Nebraska, to discuss ways to improve relocation services among their people. One participant suggested that tribal meetings be held once or twice a week to instruct members in budgeting and to explain how to use modern household facilities. "Many of our people do not know what these things are," he said, "and have never had running water in their house and other modern conveniences." A training program for Indians became pertinent to solving the existing relocation problems as well as in preventing future problems. Mishandling money was one such problem. Superintendent Ben Reifel, a mixed-blood Sioux, noted a tendency by relocatees to over-spend their income, thereby convincing other individuals that Indians received checks from the government on a regular basis. "Some people think that the Indian gets a regular check from the Federal Government. The salesman thinks an Indian is a good subject for the installment plan."

Congress passed Public Law 959 during the first week in August 1956, providing improved vocational training for adult Indians. Shortly afterward, vocational training became a part of the relocation program and offered three types of general services. First on-the-job training provided a twenty-four month, apprentice-type training for Indian employees. Work in factories on or near reservations trained individuals for jobs and gave them valuable vocational experience. Young Indians, especially, obtained such experience and were trained in rudimentary skills that would increase their chances for employment in urban areas.

Second, the adult vocational training program, designed for Indian adults who usually had families, provided training in specific occupational areas: carpentry, plumbing, and other related manual job skills. Program officers based enrollment selection on the past employment and school records of applicants. The program specified that applicants be between eighteen and thirty-five years of age, but older applicants were accepted if they took full advantage of the training and had a reasonable prospect of being employed in their specialty.

The third branch of the relocation program provided employment only. The direct employment subprogram provided job information and employment for Native Americans near reservations. Hence, industries were urged to locate nearby. Otherwise, program workers negotiated with employers in urban areas to hire relocatees, and the unemployed were placed where jobs were available.

The initial meeting between a potential employer and a relocatee was a crucial step. The Indian who had recently left the reservation sometimes did not make a good first impression. Tattered and threadbare clothes caused employers to pause and study Indian applicants with apprehension. The area director at Gallup, New Mexico, mentioned this point to the commissioner of Indian affairs in his report on Navajo placement activities. The director reported that the Navajos dressed in worn and torn clothes; some dressed in traditional garb; and men wore their hair long, arousing stares from people who were unaccustomed to Indians. Naturally, unconventional dress and sometimes shabby appearance hindered Indians who were looking for job and housing, or provoked derogatory comments while they shopped in stores.

The physical appearance of relocatees was less of a problem at factories located near reservations. To encourage Native Americans to seek vocational training and employment, the Bureau of Indian Affairs negotiated contracts with business firms to build plants near reservations. Bulova Watch Company built a jewel-bearing plant near the Turtle Mountain Reservation at Rolla, North Dakota, the first company to locate near a reservation and to hire exclusively Indian employees. On the last day in December 1956, the company threatened to close the installation, provoking sharp reactions. Native American leaders, as well as public officials and Indian interest organizations, urged congressmen and the BIA to retain the plant. Closing the facility would threaten the progress of the Turtle Mountain Indians and the relocation program. Bureau officials believed if all 150 Indian employees at Bulova lost their jobs other Native Americans would question the practicality and advisability of urban relocation or of receiving employment or vocational training through the relocation program. The BIA was also concerned that other industries would be reluctant to accept government subsidies for locating near reservations.

The Department of the Interior especially encouraged industrial development on and near the Navajo Reservation in the southwest. In December 1956 the Interior Department announced that $300,000 of the Navajo tribal fund was marked for creating an industrial development program. The program would induce industrial plants to locate near the Navajo Reservation, and provide payrolls and job opportunities for tribal members. Two manufacturing companies, Navajo Furniture, a subsidiary of Baby Line Furniture of Los Angeles, and Lear, a manufacturer of electronic equipment of Santa Monica, California, were each expected to employ an estimated one hundred Navajos.

The need for on-the-job experience among the Navajos was especially important because of the limited supply of jobs near reservations and the threat of layoffs to those who had jobs. Unskilled Indians had to compete with other workers in urban areas for jobs requiring specific skills. Vocational training would prepare relocating Indians for earning their livelihoods in the cities. The Indian Vocational Training Act of 1957 authorized the establishment of job training centers near reservations and in cities to teach trades to relocating Indians. The variety of training increased for several years; eventually, vocational training centers offered training in 125 occupations, and accredited schools existed in twenty-six states.

Vocational training and employment assistance for Native Americans were two primary objectives of the relocation program. The availability of employment in cities naturally led to relocation in urban areas. Hence, the need for employment became the basis for relocation. Relocation did not merely mean removing Indians from reservations to cities, but involved preparing them for placement through vocational training and moving them to areas with high employment opportunities. Public Law 959 emphasized employment for Indians, which became the main service provided by the relocation program and led to changing the name of the "relocation program" to "employment assistance." More importantly, "relocation" had become associated with the negative image of dragging Indians from reservations and abandoning them in cities. The BIA hoped the name change would improve the program's image.

The vocational training program aroused considerable interest among Indian people. The offer of free training, without necessarily having to move to some city, attracted applications. In addition, Bureau officials visited numerous council meetings to promote the advantages of vocational training opportunities. Their efforts increased Indian interest, which also meant increasing the annual cost of the entire relocation program. Congress appropriated $1,016,400.00 for the 1956 fiscal year. The expense per person amounted to $190.00. In fiscal year 1957, the total budget climbed to $3,472,000.00, at a cost of $347.20 per relocatee.

The Department of the Interior sensed a growing Native American voluntarism for relocation services, and announced on 24 July 1957 that seven hundred positions were available for on-the-job training opportunities. Federal efforts to entice industrial expansion, which would produce jobs, were successful when the BIA negotiated contracts with eight companies, including White-Tree's Workshop, an Indian-owned firm that manufactured souvenirs on the Cherokee Reservation in North Carolina. Saddlecraft, Incorporated, of Knoxville, Tennessee, intended to operate a leather-goods plant at Cherokee Reservation in North Carolina; and Lear, Incorporated, of Santa Monica, California, had already developed an electronics plant at Flagstaff, Arizona. The others included Casa Grande Mills, a garment factory in Arizona; New Moon Homes, Incorporated, of Rapid City, South Dakota, which made trailer homes near the Standing Rock Reservation; Navajo Furniture Industries, Incorporated, with a company at Gallup, New Mexico; and Bably Manufacturing Company, a denim garments factory located near the Yakima Reservation. Unfortunately these companies could hire only a small percentage of the growing number of applicants for vocational training.

Federal funding increased in correlation with the rising number of applicants until the high cost caused disagreement among federal officials. Some congressmen supported the relocation program, while others advocated the development of tribal economic resources, a less expensive route. In a confidential letter to Commissioner Emmons, dated 9 October 1957, Congressman E.Y. Berry of South Dakota complained of federal spending on Indian relocation. "I think the time has come to stop this useless waste of the taxpayers' money in hiring an army of bureaucrats to do something that does not in any way benefit the Indian people," Berry wrote.

Skeptical congressmen questioned the high overhead costs. People, especially those unfamiliar with Indian affairs, wanted clarification of the goals and objectives of the relocation program, fearing that the program was getting out of control. Terminationists who wanted to get the government out of the "Indian business" complained about the expanding and ever-increasing cost of the Bureau of Indian Affairs.

A report entitled "The Program of Relocation Services," dated 28 October 1957, reiterated the purpose of relocation. The prime directive was to assist Native Americans who wanted independence from the federal government and were eager to find their place in the free-enterprise system. The Indian citizenry, the report claimed, would eventually become a component of the urban community scene.

The relocation program reinforced the termination policy in decentralizing the federal authority in Washington. With the dispersal of federal responsibilities according to Public Law 280, the states assumed many services to Native Americans. States supplied relocation assistance that Native Americans needed. Homer B. Jenkins, assistant commissioner of Indian affairs, informed the area directors of Portland, Phoenix, Minneapolis, and Muskogee, as well as field relocation officers at St. Louis, Oakland, and Chicago, that applicants who desired vocational training should be referred to state agencies. Jenkins's order was congruent with the termination directive calling for federal withdrawal of government intervention in Indian affairs.

Indian veterans of World War II and the Korean War had a much better chance of succeeding in relocation than reservation Indians who had never left their rural communities. Previous experience with the outside world, plus the possession of knowledge of white American norms and values, accounted for this advantage. For the majority of relocatees, however, urbanization presented a difficult social and psychological adjustment to an alien environment. In early December 1957, a relocation specialist emphasized such problems in a memo to the area director of the Phoenix area office: "Relocation is not easy. It calls for real stamina and vigor, adaptability and strength of character." He added that the Papago Indians possessed these characteristics, for since 1952, 566 Papagos had successfully relocated to urban areas. Among the Navajos, Tribal Chairman Paul Jones admitted that the relocation program was helpful in removing the surplus population on the reservation that the land could not support. Frequently, tribes worked to rid their reservations of undesirable members through relocation. Shiftless, unmotivated members burdened families, friends, and reservation resources, and relocation offered them an opportunity to leave.

In summarizing Indian affairs for 1957, the Department of the Interior reported that nearly seven thousand Native Americans had received relocation assistance in finding jobs and establishing homes in urban areas. Expenditures for the relocation program in 1957 totaled 3.5 million dollars, more than twice the sum appropriated for the previous year. From the close of World War II to the end of 1957, approximately one hundred thousand Indians had left reservations. Interestingly, three-fourths of this number had relocated without federal assistance. Although reservation revenues and economic development were on the rise, with royalties from oil, gas, and other mineral leases doubling over the previous year to total more than 75 million dollars for 1957, the growing Indian population from the war boom was severely straining tribal efforts to provide for all the people.

Relocation climaxed between 1952 and 1957, when over 17,000 persons received services. About 12,625 people were resettled in cities, many of whom were living there with their families. The average cost per relocatee amounted to $403.00. The Chicago field relocation office reported for February and March 1957 that the average male relocatee earned $1.60 an hour, or about $66.00 for a forty-hour week. To maintain services for Native Americans, a total of twelve relocation offices were in operation across the country.

The rising demand for relocation was temporarily jeopardized during the economic recession of 1956-57, when jobs became scarce and cutbacks in production occurred. Employers usually laid off relocatees first, due to their lack of job experience or seniority. As a result, for fiscal year 1958 the number of relocatees decreased by 1,236, or about 18 percent, from the previous year. To survive their economic ills, many Indians of terminated trust status sold their lands at depressed prices. The drop in applications was brief; interest returned the following year, and on 1 April, the BIA reported a surplus of 3,000 applicants. And so the deluge of Indians moving to the cities continued.

Unfortunately, many potential relocatees did not anticipate the difficulties that they might encounter in the cities. Louis Cioffi, a missionary, wrote to President Eisenhower: "Under the program, as you know, Indians are urged away from their reservations, given jobs, which soon come to an end. As you may not know, many have returned to the reservation, discouraged and worse off than before. Successful relocation achieved by the government has been very small indeed." One Indian in Southern California called relocation an "extermination program," and said that Eisenhower believed "the Indians would be integrated by taking all the youngsters off the reservation, the old would die off, the young would be integrated, and the land would become free for public domain, and all the people could grab it."

Conversely, the government reported optimistically that the majority of Indian relocatees were acclimating to urban conditions successfully, and the number returning to reservations was actually minuscule. The Bureau of Indian Affairs maintained that between 1953 and 1957 only three out of ten relocatees returned to their home communities. The BIA claimed that one half of those 30 percent who returned home did so within the first three months, and that 71.4 percent remained in their urban environment. Critics charged that percentage of returnees was 75 percent. Such differences in statistics helped to fuel the controversy over the relocation program. In fact, both sides probably manipulated figures to favor or disfavor the "return rate."

Another problem area arose when vocational training programs encountered a significant dropout rate in various occupational areas. In the nurse's aide program the rate was 21 percent; for sawmill workers 50 percent; for manufacturers of Indian artifacts 54 percent; and for furniture workers about 62 percent. Specialized occupations, such as diamond processing, wig-making, and the production of women's fashion items, had the highest dropout rates, due to the monotony of the work. Most likely, a disinterest in the work and its long-range impracticality accounted for the high dropout rate in wig-making and the production of women's fashion items. Often, the relo-catees were persuaded to enroll in a number of widely ranging cour-ses, merely to prove that Indians were being trained in diverse occupations.

Monotony and disinterest were not the only reasons why Indians dropped out of vocational training programs. Frequently, relocatees were placed in seasonal jobs, like agricultural work, and in other jobs that lacked employee security. For these reasons, relocatees became suspicious of government officials who ostensibly would find jobs for them. Unfortunately, low wages accompanied these insecure jobs, forcing Indians to gravitate toward poor housing areas in the cities. In Los Angeles, Indian families were placed in slum dwellings and in rundown motor courts. As more families moved to these areas, Indian ghettos developed. Frustration and discouragement compounded homesickness, prompting many to leave the cities.

Other relocatees chose to return because they missed the "open-ness" of their reservations. Some left well-paying jobs just to return home. In a few cases, however, if a family member died in an apart-ment the other members of the family did not want to stay because it was taboo to continue living there. One relocatee had a bad dream and decided to go back to the reservation. Relocation officers thought that these reasons were only excuses to leave. What they failed to understand was that bad omens and taboos were a part of the Indian reality and affected behavior accordingly. Other Indian urbanites found modern institutions too overwhelming; in buying on credit, for example, their inability to make installment payments created indebtedness, possibly even bankruptcy.

Racism was another serious problem confronting relocatees in some areas, although Indian-white relations had improved in general. A 1958 "Report of the Labor Force and the Employment Conditions of the Oneida Indians" revealed that discrimination against the Oneidas in northern Wisconsin had declined. Urban communities surrounding the Oneida Reservation, like Green Bay, Appleton, and Neenah, hired Indians on a regular basis, but employers were now selective in their hiring practices because of the Indians' high rates of absenteeism from previous jobs.

A social services director of the Minneapolis Native American Center depicted the Native American hopes and disillusionment with the relocation experience: "I think everybody who comes to the city has a dream, a dream of making it, a dream about improving their lives. But then prejudice slaps them right in the face and they're worse off. Call it culture shock. When your bubble is burst, there's nothing left but to go back home and start dreaming again."

After failing to adjust to urban life and returning to the reservation, the relocatees at least had some job experience for a potentially better livelihood. Many chose to attempt relocation a second or a third time, selecting a different city for each move. Periodically, such opportunistic Indians took advantage of the relocation program and went to different cities for a couple of months on adventurous vacations. Upon returning, they boasted to friends about their good times in Los Angeles, Chicago, or whatever city they had visited.

Although relocation officers were flexible in accepting applicants, not all were easily approved. Reasons for rejection included records of drunkenness, arrests, marital problems, and poor health. Upon resolving these problems, however, Native Americans could have their applications reconsidered. In some instances, relocation officers were criticized and charged with racism for disqualifying certain applicants. But the prejudice was not always directed against Indians. John Dressler, a wise and elderly Washo, stated: "I think the Indian people also is prejudiced against the white people because of the mistreatment that they've had. I don't know who's right, whether the Indian's right or the white man's right." Dressler advised that Native Americans should try to prove themselves to be as "hearty, diligent people as they used to be" in order to eliminate poor opinions of other races. In fact, the Washo elder believed that prejudice was mutually practiced. "But in order to eliminate any kind of prejudice, I think two people have to understand each other to eliminate it," Dressler concluded. Cooperation between the two races was essential, both for improving relations between the two peoples and for the successful placement of Indian Americans in urban areas.

Relocation centers varied in their success in carrying out their difficult tasks. Several factors caused the ineffective administration of the relocation program. Most relocation officers were non-Indians who lacked a sound understanding of Native American cultures, thus preventing them from comprehending traditional behavior patterns. Some had worked previously with the War Relocation Authority, which had displaced Japanese Americans during World War 11, and they proved to be insensitive to Indian needs and problems. In addition, some offices lacked staffs sufficient to handle the large number of relocatees. Shortages in adequate housing added to the problems, and efforts to stretch funds forced officials to place Indian families in slums and in downtrodden neighborhoods that were mostly populated by other racial groups.

Poor living conditions in relocation areas increased public criticism of the government. "We are going to pay the debt owed to the Indian, a debt born of broken treaties, harsh treatment, and 'Indian business' such as the morale-breaking relocation program," wrote Louis Cioffi, in a second irate letter to President Eisenhower. Another angry citizen attacked the commissioner of Indian affairs: "Mr. Emmons is optimistic about the success of his Indian Voluntary Relocation Service. I have known many Indians who have been sold this bill of goods, only to write home begging for their families who were 'provided housing' that consisted of condemned quarters where Negroes were moved out and where the mothers had to stay awake nights and fight off the rats to keep them from biting their children."

Some problems of ineffective relocation were attributed to the Native Americans' lack of marketable job skills. In November 1959, the superintendent at the Fort Apache Indian agency in Arizona reported that the low education level of White Mountain Apache applicants disqualified them for relocation. Lacking any usable skill was another reason for dismissing applicants. The superintendent said that "we feel that it would be a disservice to the applicant if he were sent to a metropolitan area on relocation when we feel sure they could not succeed." He recommended vocational training in the unskilled and semiskilled trades for the White Mountain Apaches. However, their lack of education, would hinder their potential success in adjusting to urban life. Fortunately, vocational training agreement was negotiated with Southwest Lumber Mills to assist the Indians, and a local radio station agreed to publicize relocation opportunities and adult vocational training programs.

In another report during mid-November of the same year, John C. Dibbern, superintendent of the Colorado River Agency evaluated the relocation program for tribes under his jurisdiction. The Native American's individual concept of an acceptable standard of living, he commented, was dependent on government services, and those represented a federal security blanket. A living standard acceptable to traditional Indians did not satisfy the expectations of relocation officers and the mainstream society. Citing relocation records, Dibbern noted that nontraditional Indians seeking an improved standard of living had a better education and some experience in living off the reservation; and they possessed individual qualities to ameliorate their socioeconomic status.

Dibbern listed several problems that hindered the traditional

Indians under his jurisdiction. Drinking was common among unemployed and idle persons. But numerous individuals, who took advantage of relocation services and became gainfully employed, discontinued drinking. "Illegitimate children and unmarried mothers" presented another problem, as job placement for these women was difficult, if not impossible. An additional problem involved locating nursery care for their children. "Large families proved to be troublesome: it was difficult to find employment for a father that paid him enough to support his entire family as well as to locate housing for families of six or more people. "Obesity" was also a problem, for employers tended to refuse to hire overweight relocatees—the case for many Indians of the Colorado River Indian Agency.

On 25 November 1959, Dr. Sophie Aberle, former general superintendent of the United Pueblos Agency, sent a memorandum to Commissioner Emmons about the "weak or wrong policies held by the B.I.A," in an effort to provide possible solutions for a more effective supervision of Indian affairs. Aberle attributed policy breakdowns to the difficulties experienced in relocation program. She recommended better screening and more training of applicants to reduce the large number of returnees. She noted that relocation workers processed relocatees too hastily in an effort to meet quotas and to prove the program successful. Therefore, the program seemed to be self-defeating. In brief, relocation did not offer a workable "solution" to the "Indian problem," according to Aberle, because of the high expense involved in placing people and the large number who returned to the reservations.

Dr. Aberle expressed sympathy for Native Americans as victims of federal policy, but her views and recommendations received scant attention from federal officials. The processing of relocatees was aided by Indian eagerness to apply for relocation, thereby fueling official efforts to meet quotas regardless of whether it was right or wrong to place Native Americans in urban areas. Hence, officials made every effort to place the program in a positive light. In fact, articles in Phoenix newspapers on 28 and 29 February 1960, reported that Commissioner Emmons had pronounced the relocation program successful. "About 70 per cent of the 31,259 Indians who left their reservations for Western and Midwestern cities since 1952 have become self-supporting," stated the Commissioner. The highest reported rate of successful relocations was 76 percent in 1955, and the lowest was 61 percent in 1958.

In an effort to find out for themselves, the Navajo Tribal Council established a four-member committee to survey Navajos to determine the success of the program. The committee suspected individuals of fraudulent practices and organizations of taking advantage of relocatees' difficulties; but it could not find supportive evidence. According to the Navajos, individuals and self-interest groups allegedly used the problems of relocation to denounce the BIA and the whole relocation program for their own purpose and for publicity.

Increasing criticism of the BIA forced officials to respond regularly to allegations of wrongdoing in relocation and termination. Assistant Indian Commissioner Thomas Reid attempted to enlighten the delegates of the Province of the Midwest of the Episcopal Church at Cincinnati, who inquired about the negative spiritual impact of relocation on Indians. Reid mentioned that it was well known that the majority of reservation tribes were becoming poorer each year, while their increasing populations depleted reservation resources. "In order to help the Indians in breaking out of this vicious cycle of poverty, paternalism, and despair, we in the Bureau of Indian Affairs are taking a number of constructive steps," Reid added.

The relocation program maintained a staff at forty-five agencies; nine area offices, including Alaska; and nine field offices. The adult vocational training program offered the most assistance to Indians in obtaining jobs skills. Comprehensive training opportunities had been developed, and 346 courses were approved at 130 different institutions. The courses that interested Indians included auto mechanics, welding, cosmetology, and radio and television repair, as well as stenography and typing.

In Oklahoma, relocation officers worked with a dedicated enthusiasm to place Native Americans in urban areas. They ignored assigned quotas from the Washington office, working solely from the standpoint of human welfare. In general, the Oklahoma Indians reciprocated the officials' enthusiasm, and they perceived relocation as an opportunity to improve their personal economic status. However, some full-blood Cherokees, who recalled the "Trail of Tears," and some elderly Kiowas and Comanches resented relocation as another government scheme to get rid of them.

As Americans were undergoing an overall economic adjustment to urbanization, dependency on land for a livelihood became less important. The nation's economy now rested on mechanization, which began to replace labor and enabled industrialization in urban areas to develop at a rapid pace. While industries thrived, increasing technology demanded more qualified workers. Schools, colleges, and universities supplied the training for a work force that became increasingly specialized. The relocation program offered Native Americans the opportunity to share in this development.

One of the chief objectives of the relocation program was the desegregation of the reservation Indian population. Federal officials hoped that relocation would assimilate Indians into urban neighborhoods of the dominant society. Instead, Indian ghettos soon resulted. Chicago's Uptown neighborhood is indicative of the Indians' substandard economic living conditions. Bell and Bell Gardens in Los Angeles are other examples. Such areas fostered feelings of isolation, loneliness, and estrangement for native Americans. Many resorted to alcohol to escape the competitive and social coldness of highly individualized urbanization. Marital and delinquency problems became acute; broken marriages, school dropouts, and increases in crime were so rampant that discouraged relocatees became severely depressed and sometimes committed suicide. Tragically, a people who traditionally cherished life were now broken in spirit. Many would not return home to reservations because of self-pride: they did not want to admit failure, even though relatives beckoned them to return.

As relocation continued, some program officers became sensitive to the new problems that urban Indians faced. One such official recalled her own personal experience of being alone in a large city: "Some of my first friends were the Indian people that I worked with, being alone when I first came. My children were in New York City at the time, so I came out and stayed here alone; it was school time then. They came out to join me when I found a house. But, I realized what they [the relocatees] were faced with: the big city, the traffic, the noise, the many, many people, just the strangeness of it, and how alone you could be in the midst of so many people."

A remedy for Indian estrangement in the cities was the establishment of Indian centers. For instance, St. Augustine's Indian Center and the American Indian Center, both in Chicago's Uptown neighborhood, continue to provide counseling, temporary shelter, and other assistance to urban Indians. Similar centers in other cities offer the same services as well as opportunities for socialization among traditional Native Americans, who are a communal people. Interestingly, mutual tribal concerns and interaction dissolved many barriers between tribal groups who had never before associated with each other. Increasingly, Indian Americans in urban areas have identified themselves as Indians rather than by tribal designation.

Such socialization saved the relocated Indians. In essence, the communal tradition of Indians on reservations was imitated in urban areas. Powwows, dances, Indian bowling teams, Indian softball teams, and other related activities have intensified the survival of Indians as an identifiable ethnic group in the large cities.

Those people who remained on reservations during the relocation years of the 1950s experienced considerable economic difficulty. Even though their living conditions have improved since 1945, they often paid a high price for staying in their reservation homelands. In particular, relocation perhaps resulted in less efficient leadership among reservation tribes during the 1950s. Unfortunately, those tribal members possessing the best qualifications, and who could probably have provided a more effective leadership, were apt to relocate; and after relocating, they rarely returned to the reservation to help their tribes.

Ironically, at the same time, the majority of Indians who moved to urban areas suffered socially, economically, and psychologically. In many cases, urban Indians have traded rural poverty on reservations for urban slums. Their survival in urban areas, however, yielded hope and a brighter future for their offspring. Indian youths growing up in an urban environment often become teachers, lawyers, doctors, and other professionals. It is an unfortunate fact that success in the white world is costing them the heritage of their native culture. Today, Indians continue to experience difficulties in substituting traditional values for those of a modern world: materialism and competition.

One Indian living in California summarized the Native American reaction to relocation best:

> At the very outset, we thought it would be a good thing. It would give Indians an opportunity to spread their wings and gain education and employment and generally become equal to all other men. But after about a year or two years, at the outside, we discovered that there was an ulterior motive behind the earlier relocation program. It was designed, in fact, to get all Indians off all reservations within X number of years. I think at that time, it said twenty years; since then it has been erased, however. So, then we started digging in our heels to prevent total assimilation; assimilation to the degree that we would lose our identity as Indian people, lose our culture and our [way] of living.

The Legal and Political Status of Indian People in Chicago

Sarah Gallagher
Terry Straus
Frances Oskenaniew

American Indian people in this country have a unique legal and political status. As sovereign governments, Indians negotiated treaties and agreements with the U.S. government. Today, Indian nations retain much of that original sovereignty: they occupy a status "higher than states," and have been conceptualized as "domestic dependent nations." Tribal governments regulate the internal affairs of the tribes: they have primary jurisdiction over tribal members on tribal land. They relate directly to the federal government, which is bound in that relation by the terms of treaties, agreements, and the federal constitution as interpreted by the Supreme Court. The Bureau of Indian Affairs in the Department of the Interior, by delegation of the U.S. Congress (which has constitutional responsibility) executes federal Indian policy and maintains the federal trust responsibility. The special status of Indian tribes puts them frequently at odds with the states. States with reservations, however, are bound by federal regulation as well as by Indian votes to respond at some level to Indian interests without interfering with tribal jurisdiction.

Illinois has no reservations and is not similarly bound to address Indian interests. Indians in Chicago occupy a special legal status only insofar as they are enrolled members of tribes with reservations in other states. Yet Chicago was selected by the Bureau of Indian Affairs as one of two main relocation centers (Los Angeles, California was the other) for reservation Indians in the 1950s and 60s. The "relocation program" later called "employment assistance," was established during the period when termination of trust status typified federal Indian policy. The goal of this policy was to "get the government out of the Indian business." The BIA offered grants to individual Indians to leave their reservations and seek work in selected urban areas.

Federal support for Indians in urban areas was limited to the relocation process itself. It terminated after a set period of time, after which the federal government recognized no special relationship and offered no specific services to Indians resident in urban areas. Today, as well, most health care, social service and education benefits owed by the federal government to Indian people are not available to those resident in Chicago, although federal tribal agreements do not specify reservation residence as a condition of those benefits.

A further issue is that people who identify and are identified by others as Indians may or may not be recognized as such by the federal government. "Indians" by federal definition are enrolled members of federally recognized tribes. Various tribes are not recognized. "Recognition" requires acceptance of federal guidelines: certain tribes have avoided that process, although this may mean that the tribe receives none of the benefits of the federal trust responsibility. Several tribes were terminated: members of terminated tribes not yet restored are not recognized as "Indians" by the federal government.

Some Indian people belong to un-recognized or terminated tribes. Others belong to recognized tribes but are not officially enrolled. Most tribal enrollment procedures require a minimum "blood quantum," a concept legalized in the Indian Reorganization Act of 1934. As "blood" is measured in terms of particular tribes, a "full-blood" Indian raised on a reservation whose ancestry includes more than one tribe might not meet tribal blood quantum for enrollment eligibility. In the inter-tribal urban Indian community, tribal blood quantum and thus enrollment, becomes an even greater issue than on the reservations.

In Chicago there are many Indian people who are not "Indian" in the eyes of the federal government. All Indians in Chicago are eligible for welfare and for public services available to any citizen. By and large, however, Indian people try to avoid welfare and feel that they receive better service from Indian than from public facilities.

There is an Indian Health Service Clinic in Chicago for those who can demonstrate tribal membership. Some tribes such as the Mississippi Choctaw contract with this clinic to provide at least temporary services for off-reservation tribal members. The clinic refers many clients to the Board of Health, however, since its own facilities are limited. Board facilities in turn, have occasionally refused to serve Indian people on the basis that special facilities are open to them. Not uncommonly people return to their reservations for medical care.

Another Indian organization serving the Chicago Indian community is St. Augustine's. Supported by private contributions and federal funds, St. Augustine's provides emergency assistance, counseling and referral. It also operates an Indian Child Welfare program pursuant to the 1978 Indian Child Welfare Act, ensuring tribal jurisdiction in adoption and providing family counseling. St. Augustine's also runs the Bo-Sho-Nee-Gee Drop-In Center which provides a daily meal, five days a week, counseling, and a base for those who do not have a permanent mailing address.

The American Indian Center in Chicago was the first urban Indian Center. It developed in large part in response to the needs of Indians coming to Chicago on relocation. The Social Service department at the Center provides food, clothing and furniture to those in need and serves as a referral center for Indian people seeking services. The Senior Site provides a special place for the older community members where lunch is served daily and various activities occur. The Truancy Alternative program offers tutoring and supportive counseling to children.

With respect to education, the State of Illinois receives federal funds for Indian students but the use of those funds has been problematic. Little Big Horn High School and O-Wai-Ya-Wa grade school are Indian programs associated with particular Chicago schools: Audubon School will open a Native American program this fall (1988). There is some interest in the Chicago Board of Education in Indian-related curricula for Indian and non-Indian students alike. The dropout rate for Indian students, however, remains high. It is associated with high unemployment, also a grave problem on the reservations. The American Indian Business Association an Indian JTPA (Job Training Partnership Act) program seeks to address this condition, as does the privately-funded American Indian Economic Development Association, and the associated National American Indian Federal Credit Union, but the problems are enormous and the skill level low. The Chicago Indian community is not recognized by the federal government. The policy of the Reagan administration has been to relate only to recognized tribes doing so on a government to government basis. Indians in Chicago write proposals and struggle in lobbies and courts for the minimal support they do receive: there are no annuities or special payments to members of the Chicago Indian community as such. Their numbers are small and they live in a state with no reservations. They have little power to influence state government, yet they fall within its civil and criminal jurisdiction. Certain tribes today are seeking to extend both support and jurisdiction to their off-reservation members.

With more than half of the growing Indian population of this country living in urban areas, the relationship of tribal, state, and federal governments to urban Indian communities needs to be re-evaluated.

Narrative Traditions in the
Chicago Indian Community

NAES Religion and Philosophy Class, Summer 1986

INTRODUCTION

American Indian narratives, from creation stories to everyday tales, are a conduit of tribal and community knowledge. They represent values and meanings fundamental to tribal cultures in such a way as to connect them with the life experiences of community members. Those connections become part of the stories themselves, linking them to the community and linking past, present, and future members of the community to each other.

On every reservation there is a whole spectrum of interest in and knowledge about stories, especially the old stories. Reservation life is neither uniform nor uniformly supportive of narrative tradition. Yet the stories persist, and their persistence is important to tribal identity.

Indian people who leave their reservations and live for some period of time in an urban area are even more diverse. Some choose temporarily to set aside their Indian-ness and concentrate on finding a job, feeding the family, finishing school, or whatever: many who do so will later, when life circumstances permit, reactivate their Indian and tribal identity, seeking consciously to investigate and understand it. Others who come to the city retain strong tribal identity as they come face to face with their common Indian-ness in the inter-tribal urban context.

The Chicago American Indian community includes some 16,000 Indians from some 60 different tribes. Some have arrived only recently; some were born and raised here. Most, however, still refer to the reservation as "home," visit it whenever possible, and may plan to return permanently in the future. Many vote in tribal elections, subscribe to tribal newspapers, and sustain continual contact with relatives and friends on the reservation. Indian people in Chicago belong to at least two Indian communities and participate in varying degrees in both.

The strong connection with home reservations ensures a continual input from the reservations into the Indian community in the city. Similarly, the urban community has an impact on the reservations, particularly those which are neighboring. Reservation stories come into the city with relatives, visitors and new residents; they come by mail and by phone. Under appropriate conditions, they are told there, shared with tribal members and with other Indian people. Some are expanded and clarified in this process; some are changed to better suit the urban environment; some retain their traditional form. At the same time, new stories develop in the urban community: stories concerning people, organizations, geography, and events of the community. These stories may in turn be carried back to the reservations where they are adapted and retold. On the reservation and in the city, stories maintain community boundaries, identify community leaders, recount community history, and enhance community cohesion. They are consciously associated with Indian identity. In the city, the stories reflect the dual identity of Indian people living in cities, connecting them both to their tribes and to their urban Indian community.

In the urban community as on the reservations, certain individuals are recognized for their storytelling brilliance and style, and others for their knowledge of community oral history. Those so recognized give generously of their knowledge and talents to other Indian people. Stories are not so much told as they are given. Those receiving recognize their fortune and express their gratitude in some clear way. When the authors of this paper met with four members of the Chicago Indian community recognized for their storytelling, the student who coordinated the evening prepared fry bread and corn soup for all to share and presented each of the four with a small packet of wild rice. Food and gifts are especially appropriate when the storyteller has, as in this case, been specifically invited.

Commonly, stories are exchanged among several people. Each one will pick up on another's story, adding one to it, growing from it. Each will incorporate the listeners into the web of relationships of which the story is a part, weaving into their accounts connections with each other and with listeners, each of whom they will personally address in the course of the narrative.

THE STORIES

Stories consciously identified as Indian stories abound in the Chicago Indian community today. Various types can be distinguished: They reflect both the diversity and the commonality of Indian people: some stories are tribally specific, some stories are specific to the Chicago community, and some address the inter-tribal experience. Certain popular vignettes which might be designated "ethnic Indian stories," are told in both urban and reservation communities. They are much like Polish or other ethnic jokes, except that they are told almost exclusively to and by Indian people. They refer to common Indian experiences, reservation or urban, and they make people laugh: the shared recognition of common problems brings humor and strengthens relationships. Humor is a significant aspect of all stories told by Indians. It is also a conscious part, understood by community members as identifiably Indian and evident in ageless tribal traditions as well as in contemporary ethnic portraits.

One such ethnic Indian story is about crabs, or, alternatively, angleworms. An Indian man was on the beach collecting crabs with several non-Indians, putting the crabs into a bucket he was carrying. All the other men had trouble keeping the crabs in their buckets, but the crabs stayed in the Indian's bucket. Why? They were Indian crabs: when one tries to climb up above the others, they always pull him back down again.

Another story familiar throughout Indian country is about an Indian man who went fishing by a river and saw four eyes staring at him. When he looked carefully, he found that it was a snake holding a frog in its mouth. He decided to make the snake release the frog and rewarded it with a few sips of his brandy, then he went back to fishing. A little while later, he turned around to find the same snake holding another frog and waiting for the brandy.

A final example of these brief, inter-tribal ethnic narratives specifically unites reservation and urban Indians. In this story, a group of Indians had come to the city and were looking for the Indian Center. They picked up the smell of fry bread and followed it until they were right around the corner from the Center. There they had a flat and stopped to fix it. While the car was up on the jack, another group of Indians came by, opened the hood and took the battery. "You got the wheel, we get the battery: Indians always share," one explained.

Such stories refer to "generic" Indian experience, urban or reservation, tribal or inter-tribal. The "ethnic Indian," however, represents to many a loss of tribal identity: the urban inter-tribal environment is seen as inhospitable to the maintenance of specific tribal traditions. But the stories remain. The old stories, the "traditional" stories, are old precisely because of their adaptability. They tell of experiences and values fundamental to human life, and particularly to Indian life. They have lasted precisely because they express timeless human realities, understood through the accumulated wisdom of tribal experience. They speak to a broad range of experiences and thus have persisted where other stories have been short-lived. They are told in Chicago as on the reservations, not by everyone, but by some. They may be told in English, but they are told by bilingual/bicultural individuals who know best how to translate meaning as well as words.

The old stories, stories of creation and of the ordering of the world into right relations, change little as they are told in the city, and are told under specified circumstances. However, as children who have grown up in the city are taught the old tribal stories, it may be necessary for the one giving the story to provide reference points from the urban experience to underline meaning. A Mesquakie father, for example, telling his sons a tribal story about why dogs always sniff each other, explained that they were looking for the "king dog," the one who put out a huge fire, a fire which filled a space bigger than the Los Angeles stadium. Reference to the Los Angeles stadium emphasized by drawing on the child's experience the magnitude of the fire in the story.

Inter-tribal marriages are commonly cited as a critical factor in the loss of tribal traditions both on and off the reservation. Yet Leroy Wesaw (1978) offers a different perspective. Interviewing a Potawatomi woman, a second-generation urban resident, and her husband from a Canadian tribe, he found that "She held a great store of legends, some dealing with the origin of our religion, and...it was interesting to hear her husband adding the myths of his people to make our own legends more understandable." He thus establishes the possibility that tribal traditions may be strengthened and elucidated through inter-tribal contact. The oral history of the Potawatomi which Leroy learned in Potawatomi from his own father, he has passed down in English to his own children and grandchildren, and has written for others to share. It is, of course, only a part of Potawatomi oral history. It is at the community level, not the individual level, that tribal history is passed on; each individual, each family gives what they know.

The oral history of the Chicago Indian community covers a time period of about 75 years and three generations of Chicago residents. Relocation stories tell of the experience of Indian people coming to Chicago from reservations, independently or on federal relocation, decades ago or just yesterday: they share themes of confusion and misunderstanding, of disorientation and disappointment. But the stories are almost always humorous.

An Oneida man, a long term Chicago resident, laughs at himself and tells about his discovery of television upon arriving in Chicago. It was so fascinating to him that he used to sit and watch it even after it was turned off, watch it until the little white dot on the screen finally disappeared. One day, he was watching television and some of his friends came by to visit. They didn't like the particular show he was watching and asked to change the channel. Channel? He had no idea about channels and witnessed in amazement the selection of a new show as one friend ran through the other programs airing simultaneously.

A young Oneida and Sioux girl arrived in Chicago a month ago with her mother. She was fascinated by how far the people had to jump to get down to the street when she first got off the elevated train. She didn't realize there were stairs. Flights of stairs and elevators were and are a new experience for many upon arriving in the city. The height of buildings in general was astonishing: skyscrapers absolutely overwhelmed. In some cases, even buses came in two stories. Clothing was different in the city: blue jeans were not acceptable dress for many jobs, and new residents in the city often learned this the hard way and laughed at it later on.

A Chippewa man who came to Chicago alone on federal Relocation was recruited by a federal agent on his (Lac Courtes Oreilles) reservation when he was just eighteen years old. He and another young man were scheduled to leave together, lending support to each other as they travelled to and first encountered the city. At the last minute, however, the other young man decided not to go, so Henry left his home alone and with no real concept of where he was going or how he would live.

Boarding school stories often contain much the same sense of displacement. They are told by anyone old enough to have attended Indian boarding schools during the time when those schools served expressly as vehicles of assimilation. "If we spoke Indian, we were strapped. Once ..." and so on. Stories of running away from boarding school are very common. A Sioux man tells, for example, of running away often from the BIA boarding school in Ft. Yates, North Dakota, to his home twenty-seven miles away. He and his friends were chased by police across the cornfields, but they were never caught. A Winnebago man describes running away from the boarding school he had attended in northern Wisconsin, running all the way to Madison where he stayed with some relatives. The image of the naive, confused Indian, struggling between two cultures is, however, complemented by tales of urban success and accomplishment, stories which tell of the valuable work of community leaders. Willard LaMere, for example, the Winnebago man who escaped from his Wisconsin boarding school, was a long-term resident of Chicago, involved in the development of many organizations in the Indian community here and a continuing influence upon it, though he recently retired to live on his wife's (Oneida) reservation in northern Wisconsin. As a prominent, older community leader, many stories remain in the community about him and about his work here.

Stories about Willard LaMere and Leroy Wesaw, like stories about Bill Redcloud (Chippewa) and Eli Powless (Oneida), other past community leaders, are stories about the development and growth of the Indian community and its organizations. The history of the organizations is told and remembered as a history of individuals and relationships: the history of the community is always and inevitably tied to individual lives and connections. Of Bill Redcloud, along with stories of his work in the community (finding jobs for Indians, helping to establish the American Indian Business Association, working at the Indian Center, and in the Chippewa Club), there are stories about his skill as a hunter, and, more generally about his life on his home (Red Lake) reservation. Dan Battise tells, for example, about driving all night from Chicago to visit Bill in his home behind the post office at Red Lake, and of being greeted upon his arrival with a magnificent "Indian breakfast" of fish, deer, and bear laid out cooked, but whole, across the table.

Eli Powless was also deeply involved in the American Indian Center. He danced and he bowled, and was variously involved in the Indian community. Many remember his old red Rambler, his cakes, and his endless good will. Many speculate today why and how he disappeared from the community. Some of his belongings are still kept by friends and neighbors.

The Indian organizations and especially the American Indian Center provide both focus and definition for the Chicago Indian community. Stories of their development, their interconnections, and their personnel are common markers of community involvement: those who know and tell them demonstrate their community connections by so doing. The physical grounds of the American Indian Center are also important in urban narratives. The building itself has touched many lives, held many prayers, and carried many stories. It has been a focus of traditional ceremonies over the last three decades, and it continues to hold the good things that come from these ceremonies. The elders of the community meet and are fed there in the senior site. Young people go to the senior site to listen and to learn from their elders, to witness the possibility of being Indian in the city, of surviving, and of remaining Indian. The building is unwieldy and inefficient, but all the good associations are a continuing support to the organization. A new place might be more efficient, but it would be less valuable, lacking the depth of history and the meanings associated with the current one.

There are other kinds of stories about the Center building, too, stories about strange occurrences late at night, stories, for example, about "Old Stovepipe," a spirit which wanders the building "looking like Abe Lincoln in his stovepipe hat." Many odd occurrences and encounters are attributed to "Old Stovepipe."

A dramatic example of how a story grows and changes with the experiences of those who hear and tell it involves "Old Stovepipe" and the authors of this paper. For purposes of this paper, the authors interviewed four recognized storytellers from the community, each from a different tribe. A Mesquakie consultant was telling about "Old Stovepipe," weaving into the story another narrative based on the

Mesquakie tradition of saving an infant's "belly button," the dried part of the umbilical cord that falls off within a week or two of birth. Children separated from their belly buttons are said to become too curious, always looking for something. Once, when he was working late and alone at the Indian Center, the Mesquakie narrator heard someone fooling with a door, rattling it and turning the door knob. Curious by nature (people teased him about his missing belly button), he went to see what was happening. Every time he went to check, the noise stopped. Once more, it seemed as if someone were rattling the door and he walked slowly, quietly up to it. Dramatizing what he did to try to catch whomever was behind the door, he reached for the doorknob. At that very moment in the narrative, the door swung open. The narrator and everyone else in the room froze. In walked two very surprised women who were late for the meeting. Laughter then took over the room.

When someone from that group retells stories of childhood curiosity or of "Old Stovepipe," the stories will have a special meaning, evoke a special laughter based on that experience. The explanation for that laughter will become part of the story itself. The old Mesquakie story and the story from the American Indian Center are both still there, but each has grown by association with the other, and by the particular experience of the door actually opening in the context of one man's telling of the story.

Old Stovepipe has been associated with the Indian Center building for many years. NAES College, on the other hand, has occupied its new location for only three years. Within the last year, several staff members have reported seeing a stout woman wandering through certain rooms on the first floor of the building, a spirit which disappears when it is followed. Now, when something is missing or something goes wrong, "that lady" is often jokingly blamed for it. She has become part of the lore of the organization.

There are many such stories about unusual occurrences and specifically about encounters with spirits. Such stories tell of experiences which are understood by community members as in some way identifiably Indian.

Also defined as "Indian" is a special respect for and relationship to the surrounding natural world. In every Indian community there are stories about prominent or special geographical features. In Chicago, Lake Michigan receives the greatest narrative attention, although there are also stories associated with other natural features such as forest preserves and rivers. The Indian canoe club navigated both the lake and the Chicago River, providing cultural education, community activity and adventure for Indian youth associated with the Indian Center. The canoe club no longer meets but stories of skill, valor, and excitement surround its various races and outings.

Besides canoeing, the lake is regarded as a good place for gathering during the warm weather. A story about one such gathering reveals the unfortunate public ignorance of Indian people: an Indian Alcoholics Anonymous group was having a Celebration of Sobriety picnic by the lake one afternoon. There were many people playing radios, bongos, and other instruments by the lake, but when the Indian group began to sing around their drum, the police arrived to ask for their permit. In the end, the group phoned a friend in the police department who straightened out their right to gather and to sing and, indeed, many non-Indian people of various races and nationalities joined them around the drum. The lake is also thought of as a good place to sit quietly and think. Indian people also go to the lake to pray, offering a pinch of tobacco when that is possible.

Animals stories, especially hunting stories, are very popular in Chicago. Many are "back home" stories which tell of reservation experiences, but city fauna, dogs, cats, squirrels, birds, have their own stories.

While connections to the natural world feature prominently in Chicago Indian stories, Indian people also laugh at the romantic elaboration of Indian nature lore evident in the white imagination. Kinsella's wonderful, fictional description of interchange between a white woman and an Indian man at a funeral gathering might just as well have taken place in Chicago:

> Most white people don't see Indians up close too often, so when they do they ask lots of questions, most of them silly. A big white lady in a purple dress that about seven sizes too small ask Rider Stonechild if he can tell how the weather, she say she hear all Indians can tell how good or bad a winter we going to have by signs in nature. When Frank hear that, he push right in front of Rider Stonechild, put his hand on the fat lady's big, blotched arm and say, "I am Duck's Breath; hunter, guide, car salesman, and weather forecaster. For $20 I will tell you all my secrets."

> "Well, I'm not sure I want to pay," say the white lady, and she look suspicious at Frank. "Do you forecast weather by the way animals store food, and grow winter coats?"

> "Wish I could grow a winter coat," says Frank. "Nice full length leather is what I'd grow. Instead I got to steal from the Goodwill Store. But I use the rock method to forecast weather."

> By this time he got half a dozen white folks around him. "I take this little rock, nice and smooth, weigh maybe a pound. I tie a string around it, hang it from a fence rail. If the stone is wet, it's

raining. If it's dry, it ain't. If it's swinging, it mean the wind is blowing. If there's a shadow under it, that mean the sun is shining. If it's white on top, that mean it snowed. For only $20 each I could teach you guys how to forecast like that." That ain't very funny, but what is funny is that white people don't know whether to believe him or not. If a white person said what Frank did, everyone would laugh and say, "How silly." It never occur to them that us Indians have a sense of humor.

All the stories teach values. Values identified in the stories told by consultants for this paper were: concern for the youth of the community; respect for nature, for prayer, for elders, for warriors and veterans; the importance of sharing, of encouraging and helping one another, and the importance of education, learning from relatives and elders in both communities, and using that education to serve others. Indian parents and other relatives make great use of stories in teaching values and behaviors to their children. NAES students participating in this study identified their own use of stories to teach their children as supportive of their Indian identity. Some of the stories they teach to their children are stories that scare; some are stories that provide examples, models of both good and bad behavior. Of the stories that scare, many include threatening non-human beings, bogey-man types which take or harm young children. Some parents in Chicago adapt reservation bogey-man stories to the Chicago environment. One mother from the Cheyenne River (Sioux) Reservation, for example, notes:

A story that was told to me as a young child was told when we used to go after wood late in the afternoon to cook the evening meal. There were others included in these stories because we all live in the same place. The story:

There were some little people who lived in the woods who would take and eat little children, so we had to stay right beside whoever took us to the woods with them. Sometimes these little people would make a person go crazy, but most of the time it was a little old lady all dressed up in black that sat by the tree stump with her big ax and waited for fat little kids. We were made to actually look for this little old lady and we used to think that we actually saw the person. So we would stay right beside our grandma or aunt whichever took us to gather the wood.

This is how I changed the story for my daughter while in one of the forest preserves; there are some little tiny people who live in those woods, you can't see them because they hide from adults and only little kids can see them (this is part of the original story) and if you go wander into those woods they will find you and eat you up and your mom will never know what happened to you. This story I tell to my daughter in hopes that she too will listen and be cautious as she grows older and to keep the traditions, but most of all the important part of that story is so that she does not wander too far into the trees herself because she will get lost, and that she will stay by some adult most of the time.

The bogey-man is relocated from Cheyenne River to Chicago to serve the purpose (s)he has always served, teaching little children not to wander too far from their parents, especially not into the woods.

Another "monster" which had to adapt to the urban environment is described by a Winnebago woman. On the reservation, such beings are said to inhabit bodies of water, especially spring-fed ponds or lakes, and are known to have injured or even killed tribal members who encounter them. Such beings have been encountered in Chicago, but here, they inhabit the city sewer system. Tribal stories, trickster tales, for example, and, for at least one Chippewa mother who participated in this paper, stories of Mah Kunce (cub bear) are also used to instruct and to warn young children. She comments, "Being that my children are practicing Catholics, I incorporate various aspects of the ten commandments into story telling, involving the Great Spirit as he relates to Mah Kunce. I had to adapt to these measures for Chicago, as we have no Chippewa resources to gain this lesson from."

A Winnebago and Mesquakie woman comments:

My children do not respond to oral reprimand positively unless they are accompanied or followed by a story. My stories are not usually mythological concerning trickster, but are effective because they are stories concerning fragments of my life, their life at a young age, or a relative. For example, if they are feeling the pressures of teenage love, I tell why I can relate to them because of my adolescent family and behavior problems, or of something that happened to a close friend. I like to share with them not preach at them. If I feel they need to be inspired to be more assertive or aggressive I tell then of their grandfather who was a boxer for the navy. I also share many humorous or traditional things about our family that were or are done. That way, when exposed to Indian mannerisms, it won't be alien to them.

I became aware of how my children learn by humor and gossip I share with my friends about relationships and people—especially my six-year-old and fourteen-year-old who like to listen to my telephone conversations.

My children love to ask me to describe them in detail as babies, what they did or said that was cute, when they were sick, and how they responded to babysitters etc. I like to really butter them up when they ask me about themselves because I know I am reinforcing a positive reflection of themselves. I describe how good and generous they were. Their ears really perk up and their eyes twinkle with pride.

Contemporary stories of family life are very important.

Children thrive on experience, to learn from someone they love or even someone they don't like.

[K]ids need stories and explanations because they help them to understand better and to formulate their own opinions and answers which are the best possible ones for them in their world today. I try to instill in my children to be leaders not followers. They can't be good leaders if they don't know where to go for answers. The best way for them to have answers is to share yourself with them not as a parents but as another human being, relating to each other and trusting them to go out each day and make the right decisions for themselves.

Personal stories and stories about family members and friends are used to increase the experience of children, to give them a store of experiences to draw upon in making decisions for themselves. Such stories are also told among adults, and when they are told, it is referred to as "sharing." One person shares a part of his life, his experience, with those around him, those he cares about: in response, others contribute their own stories, thus enhancing the experience of the group immeasurably.

Personal stories are commonly used to emphasize and clarify a particular point. In Chicago as elsewhere, certain community members are known for being wordy, taking a long time to "come to the point." In each case, the "wordiness" consists of detailed personal narrative, intended to underline the significance of what is being said.

Personal narrative is also prominent in what might be called "introduction." When an Indian person—in the city or on the reservation—is called upon to speak publicly, he/she will usually begin with a personal narrative which establishes his right to address the group. This was illustrated at the recent Chicago Indian Community Organization Conference where each of the main speakers began with a personal narrative which related him/her to his/her own ancestors, to those present, and to others in the community.

Interpersonal introductions also include personal narrative. During conversation among Indians here, the mention of someone's name is often followed by a narrative description of that person, who (s)he is, what is his/her relationship to the speaker, where (s)he came from, what (s)he has done here, and so on. It is a story itself apart from the original conversation. Much that may already be known in the reservation community where the population is fairly stable and everyone knows everyone else, is communicated in such narratives in the urban community.

The place of gossip in the Indian community is perhaps best understood in the context of personal stories. Gossip, recognized as a potent force of social control and political action in reservation communities, is equally significant in the urban Indian community. Gossip is the telling of everyday personal stories embellished with fantasy and personal interest. The central topics of gossip revolve around drinking, sex, and money. Community leaders are expected to be role models for the community and their behavior in these regards is closely scrutinized, as is that of their relatives. Fear of gossip thus has its positive influence. It also divides organizations and misdirects administrative decisions. Members of the community have been enough concerned about the disruptive aspects of gossip that they have sponsored and participated in gossip workshops. (Tapes of these workshops are on file in the NAES Library and Resource Center.)

CONCLUSION

It is clear that stories and storytelling are highly valued in the Chicago Indian community today. While there is a spectrum of interest and attention, the relevance of the stories to Indian and tribal identity is clearly acknowledged. Some of the stories told in Chicago originate on the home reservations of community members. Traditional stories of creation and the ordering of the world describe fundamental relations and change little as they move to the city, though the storyteller may include interpretive references which help to set the story in a relevant frame. Other tribal stories, tales of tricksters or monsters, and stories told to teach children, may be changed in various ways to suit the urban environment. "Back home" stories about reservation people, places, and activities help to inform the young and secure the tribal identity of the narrator. Relocation stories reflect differences between reservation and urban Indian life, while "ethnic Indian" stories are evidence of commonality. New stories, of course, arise in the urban community, and many of these reflect values and experiences as identifiably Indian.

In the urban setting, narrative traditions encompass both "home" and "here," past and future: they are critical to the maintenance of both tribal and Indian identity and they are consciously embraced as such by those in the community who think about such things.

Chicago's Native Americans
Cheechakos, Old-Timers and Others in the City of the Wild Garlic

Virgil J. Vogel

Several years ago a student reporter for the Truman College *Word* interviewed the director of the American Indian Center at 1630 Wilson Avenue. The director apparently played a little joke on the reporter, who wrote: "There are over 100 Indian tribes represented in Chicago, the most predominate [sic] being the Cheechako." There is no Cheechako tribe. Cheechako is Chinook jargon, meaning "newcomer," which is widely used in Alaska to describe a "greenhorn," or in western lingo, "a tenderfoot."

This incident illustrates how poorly informed whites are about Native Americans and how easily they are misled. Let us learn some basic facts about the first Americans in this city of the wild garlic.

There is no dependable count of their numbers in the Chicago area, but guesses range from 16,000 to 20,000. The city ranks next only to Los Angeles and San Francisco among large cities, in the number of reported Indian residents. More than ninety-five percent of them have come here, or are children of those who have come here, since 1951. The precipitating cause of their migration was the Indian Relocation program launched in that year under pressure of Congress. Indians were given short-term financial assistance if they would move from reservations to the city for "better economic opportunity." Opponents of the program, such as Roosevelt's Indian commissioner John Collier, charged that relocation was just a gimmick to shift responsibility for the Indians from the federal government to local taxpayers. City Indians lost medical and other benefits available to reservation Indians. Some of these benefits stem from nineteenth century treaties in which Indians surrendered most of their lands to the government. Supporters of relocation said it was intended to "open doors" of opportunity for the Indians. Alternative proposals to help make life economically viable in reservation communities were dismissed by a government anxious to "terminate" the Indian tribes and release itself from treaty obligations. The "open door" of relocation, for many, led only to skid-row, welfare, alcoholism, and broken families. It is estimated that more than a third of relocated Indians went back home after less than a year's taste of urban life. However, enough of them remained to establish a noticeable Indian presence in Chicago and other relocation cities. Relocation was abandoned in 1972, but poverty continued to drive Indians to the cities.

To aid in the adjustment of relocated Indians to the strangeness of urban life, a Chicago Indian Center was organized in 1953, with the assistance of the Bureau of Indian Affairs. Its first location was at 411 N. LaSalle St. Aside from a small Indian and white organization called Indian Council Fire, dating from 1923, the Center was Chicago's first organization for Indians, and the first to provide any services. Today there are more than a dozen organizations in Chicago which serve Indians, but the Center remains the most important. In 1963 it moved to 738 W. Sheridan. Four years later a bequest enabled the Center to buy its present building, a former Masonic hall at 1630 Wilson Ave. This institution was a major reason why many Indians clustered about Uptown and adjacent neighborhoods. It was a place where children could play basketball and enroll in summer day camps, where adults could hold educational and social activities (including weddings) and receive advice and referrals on problems of employment, housing, and welfare.

The Center has had a stormy history, including factional fights, splits, insolvency, and instability, especially in the period immediately following the death of its director of twelve years, Robert Rietz, in 1971. Rietz was a white man with an MA in anthropology from the University of Chicago, who worked well with an almost entirely Indian board of directors composed of fifteen members. Eventually the Center's problems were overcome, and it is now headed by Matthew Pilcher, a Winnebago Indian. The Center is serviced by a small professional and volunteer staff supported by dues, the proceeds of annual pow-wows, by the United Way, and by private grants. During the last fiscal year, it serviced nearly 7,000 people, some of them non-Indians.

Of the dozen or more institutions which now serve the city's American Indians, most are located in Uptown and nearby areas. These include St. Augustine's Indian Center, an Episcopal church agency founded in 1958 by Father Peter Powell, at 4512 N. Sheridan, and its Drop-In Center at 4420 N. Broadway; the Native American Committee, directed by Florence Dunham, at 4456 N. Hermitage; the Native American Educational Services, 2838 W. Peterson; and the Native American Health Service, at 838 W. Irving Park Road.

Indians are the lowest ranking ethnic group in nearly all statistical measurements of social and economic well-being. This includes life expectancy, infant death rates, unemployment, years of schooling, and average income. While conditions are improving, the lag is still there. Another problem, brought to Indians by whites, is alcoholism. The various symptoms of social decay are evident in Uptown where the largest number of the city's Indians reside. A Chicago police officer once told a reporter: "We didn't get them all with bullets and smallpox-infected blankets, but we're gonna get them with Uptown."

Indians, however, organized to fight back. Some who were dissatisfied with the often cautious and faction-ridden service organizations formed more militant groups. One of these was the Chicago Indian Village, organized by Mike Chosa, a Chippewa from Lac Du Flambeau, Wisconsin. It was formed after a Menominee Indian mother and her six children were evicted from their apartment. The Chicago Indian Village seized the occasion to agitate for better housing. For several weeks in 1970 they maintained a tent colony along the railroad tracks near Wrigley Field, opposite the eviction site. When they were expelled from that location they moved to a Nike missile site near Belmont harbor in Lincoln Park, from which they were forcibly ejected in a fierce pre-dawn raid by the police. Subsequently they camped at several rural locations near Chicago, until they dissolved in 1972.

The Minneapolis based American Indian Movement, famous for its occupation of Wounded Knee, South Dakota, in 1973, was never strong here, but the Native American Committee, formed in 1969, made the defense of Indian rights its main activity. Today it is more a service agency similar to the Center. One of its offshoots is the Native American Educational Services, once affiliated with Antioch College, which became a separate institution in August, 1985. Presided over by Faith Smith, a Chippewa, it offers college training for Indians in this city and at three reservation locations.

The University of Illinois at Chicago has an Indian Studies Program. Truman College occasionally offers Indian courses, and has a state funded Institute for Native American Development whose stated purpose is "to provide Native Americans with assessment, vocational training, and supportive services."

Indian dissatisfaction with the treatment of their children in Chicago public schools led to a demand for an Indian high school. In 1973 the Chicago Board of Education funded such a school, called Little Big Horn School (for the Custer defeat of 1876), at several successive locations, the latest being Senn High School. Its co-ordinator is Lucille St. Germaine, a Winnebago-Chippewa. The O-Wai-Ya-Wa Resource Center at Goudy School, 5120 N. Winthrop, has a small staff servicing the needs of Indian pupils at a half dozen grade schools.

All of the above reportage fails to convey the human side of being an Indian in Chicago. Newly arrived Indians undergo a cultural shock worse than that experienced by immigrants from abroad. For the first time in their lives they know loneliness. This is especially true of the women. Formerly they were but a short walk from friends and relatives; here they may be miles from familiar people and essential

social services, as well as jobs. It costs a dollar to ride the bus or "L".
Telephones suddenly become a necessity, and they must adapt to
white people's habits of measured time, punctuality, and the disci-
pline of the work place. Most trying of all perhaps is the chilly, imper-
sonal quality of human contacts. They complain that everyone, from
the bus driver to the school teacher, treats them as objects rather
than persons. Men without marketable skills must undergo the
exploitation and indignity of temporary low-wage employment at the
day labor agencies which flourish in Uptown. They may be victimized
by criminals and con-men, and must pay high rents for poorly maintained living quarters. They and their children do not relish being
addressed as "Chief" and the like. Indians prefer to live among other
Indians, although tribal origins differ. Generally they do not yearn for
assimilation into the dominant society. They accept the material and
technological progress, yet cling to elements of their Indian culture.
Among young and old there is increased inter-tribal nationalism and
ethnic pride, interest in the preservation of Indian culture, languages,
and the maintenance of some traditional customs. Ties to their old
reservation homes remain strong, and they love to return there for
visits.

We began with the observation that most Chicago Indians are
"Cheechakos." No one really knows the tribal origins of most of our
city Indians, but it is possible on the basis of surface observations and
materials from the service agencies to determine that the majority
comes from nearby states. Prominent among them are Chippewas
(Ojibwas) from Wisconsin, Michigan and Minnesota, Ottawas from
Michigan and Ontario, Potawatomis from Wisconsin, and Michigan,
and Winnebagos from Wisconsin and Nebraska. Also, there are Sioux
(Lakotas), mainly from South Dakota, and a few Mesquakies (Foxes)
from Iowa. We have Cheyennes from Montana and Oklahoma. From
the south come a number of Choctaws from Mississippi and Oklahoma, and a few Seminoles. There are Cherokees, mainly from Oklahoma, as well as Navajos and Apaches from Arizona, and small number of Pueblos of New Mexico.* Still others come from the Comanches
and Poncas of Oklahoma, the Omahas of Nebraska, and the Crees of
Canada. There are even a few Aleuts and Eskimos from Alaska. Anyone familiar with history recognizes these as names from a proud
past. The total number of tribes represented is estimated from eighty
to a hundred. Due to intermarriage a considerable number of our
Indians are of mixed tribal origin, and many are less then full blooded
Indian. However, the term "Indian" or "Native American," both of
which are used by the native people, is better defined in cultural than
genealogical terms. In contrast, though most Mexican Americans
have a high degree of Indian blood, few of them retain elements of

Indian culture.

The number of Indians in Chicago and in the nation (over a million) seems dwarfed by the number of other ethnic groups, and their political power is almost non-existent. However, their numbers are increasing faster than those of most other groups, and they are slowly developing a stratum of educated and professional people with leadership potential. Indians in recent years have ceased to be inert and voiceless, and native spokespeople, including women such as Ada Deer of the Menominees, have risen to provide leadership. The books of Vine Deloria, Jr., a Sioux (*Custer Died for Your Sins*), have helped to solidify Indian attitudes. We may expect that Indians will gradually experience increased social, political and economic influence.

It is time for the majority of Americans to learn more about their Indian neighbors, and to support measures designed to assist them in attaining their own goals, rather than goals that we might imagine are best for them. This would not be an act of charity, but an obligation that we owe to a people whose land our ancestors took, often by dishonorable means, in order to build this country. They must no longer be a forgotten people.

*In its original publication, the *City Journal* mistakenly cited the Pueblos as being from Oklahoma, although Vogel's manuscript was correct.

Linking the Past and the Present
A Commentary on Virgil Vogel's: "Chicago's Native Americans"

Rosalyn LaPier
David Beck

"It is time," Vogel says, "for the majority of Americans to learn about their Indian neighbors." Many Chicagoans, for example, are not aware that as many as 20,000 American Indians live in Chicago today. Most histories of Chicago fail to mention Indians after the battle at Fort Dearborn in 1812. However, 1812 is linked to the 1990s by a continuous American Indian presence in Chicago. Vogel describes some key events and organizations in the Indian community since the beginning of the federal Relocation program in the 1950s. His article provides useful background for further inquiry into the historic and present context of Chicago's Indian community: he creates a picture based on facts and figures, and to some degree addresses the human aspect of being an Indian and living in Chicago. Our commentary provides additional information regarding the links between past and present.

Before the 1950s, Chicago's American Indian population numbered in the hundreds. Vogel's contention that Chicago's Indian population increased dramatically because of the Relocation program is partially correct. Many Indians came to Chicago through Relocation. In addition, beginning with World War II and continuing through the Relocation era, many Indian people moved to Chicago on their own, looking for work.

As the population grew, the demand for social service agencies increased. Vogel states that the American Indian Center was the first agency created to fulfill this need. However, new evidence has been unearthed since his article was written, and it shows that other agencies preceded the Indian Center. The Indian Council Fire, for instance, served as a social service agency from the 1920s until the mid-1950s, when the Indian Center took over that function. After the mid-1930s, however, that function seems to have diminished considerably. Much of the financial support for these social services was provided by the Illinois Federation of Women's Clubs, a non-Indian organization which has helped support American Indian organizations in Chicago since the early 1920s. Other earlier organizations included the North American Indian Mission founded by Willard LaMere in 1947, and the American Indian Service.

Through the 1960s and 1970s, Vogel continues, additional

organizations were created to help Indians adapt to city life and solve various social problems within the community. Many of these organizations continue to operate; an updated list is provided below.

Although numerous agencies provide health, education, and welfare services, many Indian concerns in these and other areas remain unmet. During the 1970s, the activists Vogel mentions brought to public attention many of the issues and concerns of the Indian community. The public is likely to remember the protests of these activists, but Indian activism in Chicago has a long history. It dates at least to the 1893 World's Fair when Simon Pokagon, the Potawatomi leader, wrote the *Red Man's Greeting*, a bitter denunciation of the treatment of Indians by the "pale-faced race." Dr. Carlos Montezuma, a Yavapai physician and perhaps the strongest Indian activist in Chicago's history, practiced medicine in Chicago from the late 1890s until the early 1920s. He aided individual Indians in Chicago, helping people find jobs if they lived in the city, meeting them at railroads if they were passing through, or helping them return home if they were stranded here. He also fought for Indian rights nationally by attacking the Federal Indian Bureau (which became the Bureau of Indian Affairs in 1947). He did this through the Society of American Indians, a national organization, and through *Wassaja*, a newspaper he published in Chicago.

In 1923, the year Montezuma died, the Indian Council Fire (originally called the Grand Council Fire of American Indians) organized. Beginning with the Council Fire, activism and social service developed within institutions, rather than through individuals. Activists often created these institutions. For instance, the activists of the 1970s created organizations in their efforts to bring about change. Some of these organizations created by the activists, including the Native American Committee and NAES College, became social service agencies which continue to address issues such as education, housing, and employment.

Vogel does not entirely "convey the human side of being an Indian in Chicago," but he does describe the impressions the city makes on a newcomer, by listing experiences common to all migrants to Chicago. These could apply to nearly any immigrant group. He finishes the description with impressions specific to Indians. He describes the problems encountered by migrants, but not those faced by long-term residents of the city.

A work that does help convey the human side of being Indian in Chicago is the soon-to-be-published narrative edited by Donald L. Fixico with the assistance of Lucille St. Germaine, *Native Voices in the City: The Chicago American Indian Oral History Project*. This work is based on the 1983 Oral History Project sponsored by NAES

College and the Newberry Library. *Native Voices* describes life in the city from the perspective of twenty four elders in the community. Another way of learning about the Indian community from community members is by having someone come speak to your school or classroom. This can be arranged through the Information and Assistance Center at NAES College.

On a number of points of interpretation we differ with Vogel. His statement that cultural shock for Indians "is worse than that experienced by immigrants from abroad" is likely true as it relates to many immigrants from westernized cultures. We question whether it holds for immigrants from cultures significantly different from the United States, however.

Furthermore, it may be true that few Mexican Americans retain elements of their Indian culture; however, the artwork in the murals of Mexican-American communities such as Pilsen in Chicago show definite Indian influences. "Indigenismo," or pride in Mexico's Indian heritage, was one form of cultural expression that the Mexican government, under Obregon, encouraged and financed after the revolution; it has been brought to Chicago.

Finally, the statement that "No one really knows the tribal origins of most of our city Indians" may apply to organizations or agencies trying to count or categorize Indians; however, the individuals themselves for the most part do know their own tribal origins, and even bureaucratic statisticians recognize this, as indicated by a study conducted by NAES College in conjunction with the Chicago Board of Education during the 1985-86 school year. (Results of this study are available in the Community Archives of NAES College.)

The history of Indians in Chicago is complex and diverse. Virgil Vogel's article begins to explore it in the period after the 1950s, when Chicago's Indian population grew dramatically. His article is a good starting point for understanding that history. At the same time, we should remember that the history of Indians in Chicago does not stop between the battle at Fort Dearborn and the Relocation era, but flows continuously through time.

Vogel rightly complains about "how poorly informed whites are about Native Americans and how easily they are misled." The editors of his article vividly illustrated this point by mistakenly placing the Pueblos of New Mexico in Oklahoma, although Vogel's original manuscript had it correct. Virgil Vogel has spent his career trying to correct problems like these on a local and national level. This is a goal we all must strive to achieve.

Chicago American Indian
Community Organizations

All Nation Assembly of God
1126 West Granville Ave.
Chicago, IL 60660
(312) 637-2764

American Indian Artists Guild
4151 N. Ashland
Chicago, IL 60613
(312) 975-7680

American Indian Business Association/
Job Training and Partnership Act
4753 North Broadway, Suite 700
Chicago, IL 60640
(312) 784-2434

American Indian Center
1630 West Wilson Avenue
Chicago, IL 60640
(312) 275-5871

American Indian Center Truancy
  Alternative/
Optional Education Program
1630 West Wilson Avenue
Chicago, IL 60640
(312) 275-5871

American Indian Center Senior Citizens
  Program
1630 West Wilson Avenue
Chicago, IL 60640
(312) 275-5871

American Indian Economic
  Development Association
2838 West Peterson Avenue
Chicago, IL 60659
(312) 784-5505

American Indian Health Service of
  Chicago Inc.
838 West Irving Park Road
Chicago, IL 60613
(312) 838-9100

Anawim Center
1020 Leland Ave

Chicago, IL 60640
(312) 561-6155

Indian Council Fire
c/o Newberry Library, D'Arcy McNickle
  Center
60 West Walton
Chicago, IL 60610
(312) 943-9090

Institute for Native American
  Development
Truman College
1145 West Wilson Avenue
Chicago, IL 60640
(312) 989-6206

Little Big Horn High School
Senn High School
5900 N. Glenwood Ave.
Chicago, IL 60660
(312) 989-3580

D'Arcy McNickle Center for the
History of the American Indian
Newberry Library
60 West Walton
Chicago, IL 60610
(312) 943-9090

NAES College
2838 West Peterson Ave.
Chicago, IL 60659
(312) 761-5000

NAES College Bookstore
2838 West Peterson Ave.
Chicago, IL 60659
(312) 761-5000

NAES College Information and
  Assistance Center
2838 West Peterson Avenue
Chicago, IL 60659
(312) 761-5000

NAES College Library and Resource
  Center

(Community Archives)   Indians
2838 West Peterson Ave.   4512 North Sheridan Road
Chicago, IL 60659   Chicago, IL 60640
(312) 761-5000   (312) 784-1050

Native American Support Program   St. Augustine's Center
University of Illinois at Chicago   Bo-Sho-Nee-Gee Drop-In Center
P.O. Box 4347   4420 North Broadway
Chicago, IL 60680   Chicago, IL 60640
(312) 996-4515   (312) 878-1066

O-Wai-Ya-Wa Resource Center   St. Augustine's Center
Goudy School   Indian Child Welfare Center
5120 North Winthrop   -   4506 North Sheridan Road
Chicago, IL 60640   Chicago, IL 60640
(312) 784-3533   (312) 561-8555

St.Augustine's Center for American

Based on *The 1987 Chicago American Indian Community Service Directory* with
permission from NAES College and the Information and Assistance Center.

Chronological Index of
Community History: Chicago

1833   Last treaty signed ceding Illinois lands

1886   "The Alarm" statue erected in Lincoln Park

1889   Carlos Montezuma earns medical degree from Chicago Medical College

1893   Chicago World's Columbian Exposition includes Indian Village; Simon Pokagon writes *Red Man's Greeting* as protest

1894   "The Signal of Peace" statue dedicated in Lincoln Park

1896   Dr. Carlos Montezuma sets up private medical practice in Chicago after working for several years as a physician in Indian Service schools

1899   Simon Pokagon dies (January)

1903   Lincoln Park encampment (9-26/10/1)

1904   Train wreck involving members of Buffalo Bill show, including 18 Indian entertainers from Pine Ridge; Dr. Montezuma treats survivors and pleads their case to the Office of Indian Affairs

---

1913   *Williams v. City of Chicago* case initiated in Circuit Court

1917   *Williams v. City of Chicago*. U.S. Supreme Court rules Pokagon Band of Potawatomis have no right to land reclaimed from receding Lake Michigan; continued occupancy would have been needed in order for Court even to consider case

1919   Indian Fellowship League founded

1920   Indian Fellowship League sponsors Indian Days (9-24/9-26)

Indian Fellowship League reorganizes, holds first meeting.

35 tribes represented. Indian and non-Indian membership. (10-15)

1921   Indian Day (9-23)

1922   "Indian Day" week (9-20/9-26)

1923   Carlos Montezuma dies

Ordinance presented and filed in Chicago City Council to rename Rogers Avenue between Lake Michigan and the forest preserve to "Indian Trail" (May)

Society of American Indians holds annual conference in Chicago (9-24/9-30)

Annual Indian Week Encampment at Cook County Forest Preserve at Deer Grove (9-27/9-30)

Grand Council Fire of American Indians (which later became Indian Council Fire) founded

1925   Charles Albert "Chief" Bender pitches and coaches for Chicago White Sox

1928   Chicago City Council orders preservation of "Indian Peace Treaty Tree" at corner of Caldwell and Rogers (May)

Grand Council Fire of American Indians Resolution to Mayor Thompson calling for fair treatment of Indians in history books and classrooms is read into *U.S. Congressional Record*

1929   J.L. Kraft donates Totem Pole to city of Chicago

"The Bowman" and "The Spearman" Statues at Grant Park unveiled. According to Gridley, these two statues depict Plains Indians riding on European draft horses

---

1933   U.S. Senate Bill 1413, intended to make impostors illegal, initiated by Senator Frazier at request of Indian Council Fire

1933-34 Century of Progress World's Fair includes Indian Village. First Indian Council Fire Achievement Award given at 1933 Fair

1937 Billy Caldwell American Legion Post 806 chartered (10-28)

1941 Bureau of Budget orders Office of Indian Affairs to move to Chicago "to relieve congestion in war-time Washington" (December)

1942 Office of Indian Affairs moves central offices to Merchandise Mart in Chicago. *Indians at Work* now published in Chicago (Sept. 1)

1947 Office of Indian Affairs is renamed Bureau of Indian Affairs, moves central offices back to Washington, D.C.

North American Indian Mission founded by Willard LaMere and Chief Thundercloud (November)

1948-49 Santa Fe Railroad sponsors Indian Village exhibit at Chicago Railroad Fair

1949 Meetings in Chicago Welfare Council preparatory to establishment of American Indian Welfare Council

---

1951 Federal Relocation program officially begins

1953 All-Tribes American Indian Center founded

Indian Council Fire drops social service function, Achievement Award becomes major function

1953-54 Fred Saskamoose plays for the Chicago Blackhawks

1954 1st Annual American Indian Center Pow-wow

Longhouse Organization organized

1955 All-Tribes American Indian Center incorporates, becomes

American Indian Center

1955-56   Indian Center-BIA conflict

1958   Robert Rietz hired as Director of Indian Center

          North American Indian Foundation founded

1959   Indian Days officially proclaimed by Mayor Daley (May 8-10)

1960   Advisory Committee meetings for American Indian Chicago
          Conference (February)

          NCAI Resolution authorizes University of Chicago to cooper-
          ate in study of Indian problems, leading to American
          Indian Chicago Conference (November)

1961   St. Augustine's Center for American Indians founded Ameri-
          can Indian Chicago Conference at University of Chicago
          (June 14-20)

1962   *Declaration of Indian Purpose* presented to President Ken-
          nedy (Summer)

1963   *Indian Voices* begins publication

1967   Maria Tallchief receives Indian Council Fire Achievement
          Award

1968   American Indians-United founded

          American Indians-United conference in Chicago

          Council on Indian Affairs conference in Chicago

1969   Native American Committee (NAC) formed as support group
          for Indian Rights actions throughout nation

1970   NAC incorporated as not-for-profit organization

UICC begins Native American Program

Chicago American Indian Village set up near Wrigley Field (June-July)

1971   Robert Rietz dies. Political conflict within Indian Center leads to split

Chicago American Indian Village takes over Nike Missile site, and after leaving set up camp at various other places (May-Sept)

Little Big Horn High School founded (July)

UICC begins Native American Studies Program

NCAI National Conference in Chicago

1972   O-Wai-Ya-Wa School founded

1973   American Indian Business Association organized

Center for the History of the American Indian is established at the Newberry Library

1974   American Indian Health Services founded

NAES College founded

Seven Nations Talent Search Project begun

1978   *Indian Voices* ends publication

1979   O-Wai-Ya-Wa becomes a Resource Center

Institute for Native American Development established at Truman College

---

1981   Chicago American Indian Community Organizations Conference; beginnings of CAICOC (June)

The Newberry Library hosts "Urban Indians" as its third

annual Conference on Problems and Issues Concerning American Indians today

1982   Field Museum Totem Pole erected

1983   Chicago American Indian Oral History Project begun

1984   NAES College accredited as Bachelor of Arts degree- granting institution

1986   Chicago Blackhawks draft Everett Sanipass in the first round

1987   Webber Resource Center opens in Field Museum of Natural History (June 27)

Source

David Beck, *The Chicago American Indian Community, 1893-1988: Annotated Bibliography and Guide to Sources* (Chicago: NAES College Press, 1988; distributed by Chicago Academy Press), Appendix D. With permission of the author and the publisher.

7. BIBLIOGRAPHIC ESSAY

American Indians in Chicago Since 1893:
Selected Sources
David Beck

American Indians in Chicago Since 1893:
Selected Sources

David Beck

In 1919, when the state legislature designated the fourth Friday of each September as American Indian Day in Illinois, the number of American Indian people living in Chicago was in the low hundreds. That population now numbers between twelve and twenty thousand. Numerous documents and other sources exist which help reveal this community's history. Some of these are described in this chapter. But since American Indians have a special, legally-defined relationship to the federal government and American society, we need some general background before dealing specifically with Chicago.

In 1887, with the passage of the Dawes Act (General Allotment), federal Indian policy officially underwent a change. The era of treaty-making was over. The Dawes Act gave ownership of tribal land to individual Indians. It allowed the federal government to bargain with individual Indians in land deals and to sell lands declared as "surplus." During the first thirty years following passage of this law, Indians lost more than 86 million acres, or nearly two thirds of the land they had owned in 1887.

This land confiscation was part of a larger government policy of forced assimilation of Indians into white society. Indians were expected to use their individual plots of land agriculturally, to become farmers. Another aspect of assimilation involved taking Indian children from their parents and sending them to government boarding schools, where they roomed with Indians of different tribal and cultural background. In the summertime, these children were boarded with white families; all ties with their Indian background were cut. "The Mojave Indians, they have no childrens Now ..." one Mojave man wrote to Dr. Carlos Montezuma (who will be discussed below) in 1894.

In 1898 the United States further strengthened its control over Indians by passing the Curtis Act which outlawed tribal governments in Indian territory. In fact, this control was an important goal of the U.S. policy. Even the governments of the "five civilized tribes", governments constitutionally based on the United States model, were outlawed.

United States government control extended not only over tribes but over individuals as well. It extended not only to the children who were taken from their families and cultures, but also to adults. A prohibition law forbade Indian adults to possess, sell, or consume alcohol; on reservations, federal agents sometimes had near-total control over individuals' lives, including the power to grant or deny permission to leave the reservation.

These policies of assimilation and government control were not officially reversed until 1934, when John Collier became Director of the Office of Indian Affairs under President Franklin Delano Roosevelt. For a good concise discussion of federal Indian policy, see Edward H. Spicer, "American Indians, Federal Policy Toward," pp. 114-122 in *Harvard Encyclopedia of American Ethnic Groups* (25). Excellent, indepth works on federal Indian Law are *Felix S. Cohen's Handbook of Federal Indian Law* (7) and Getches and Wilkinson, *Federal Indian Law* (10). (Full citation of resources discussed here, including location of rare sources, can be found at the end of the chapter. Refer to number in parentheses.)

When American Indians move to cities they retain most tribal rights. At the turn of the century, however, if an Indian moved to the city and took up U.S. citizenship, he or she was *denied* tribal rights by the U.S. Government. Indians who chose to retain their tribal rights were not granted the right to vote, or other rights of citizenship. (Contrary to what President Reagan said in his 1988 visit to the Soviet Union, this changed in 1924 when Indians were granted U.S. citizenship.) The government did not actively encourage Indian migration from reservations to cities during the General Allotment era as it did in the 1950s, in part because of the prevailing white belief in Indian savagery, and in part because of the assumption that Indians were members of a dying race. For an historic discussion of readings on American Indian urbanization in general from pre-Columbian times through the 1970s, see Russell E. Thornton, Gary D. Sandefur, and Harold G. Grasmick, *The Urbanization of American Indians, A Critical Bibliography* (27).

Very little is known about the hundreds of Indian people who lived in Chicago in the years before World War II. Many Chicagoans throughout the years have recognized the city's Indian heritage (visible in the city seal, statues, totem poles, and street and park names), but few have recognized the continuing Indian presence in the city. In fact, most turn-of-the-century Chicagoans' only contact with Indian people was through Indians who came or were brought to the city as entertainers or to be shown to the city's non-Indians. Included in this category are Indians who came as part of one celebration or another and set up encampments within or near the city.

For instance, an Indian village, organized by ethnologists with the help of the federal government, was part of the Midway Plaisance at the 1893 World's Columbian Exposition. This type of "displaying" of non-white peoples in the great expositions of the late nineteenth and early twentieth centuries was done to show visitors the "stages" of civilization. Non-whites were displayed as inferior peoples, as being in various stages of barbarism or savagism. Robert W. Rydell describes this function of World's Expositions in *All the World's a Fair: Visions of Empire at American International Expositions, 1876-1916* (24). Numerous 1893 guide books to the Fair, describing the purposes of the exhibitions, are available at the Newberry Library and on open shelf at the Chicago Historical Society (5, 6, 16, 19).

Simon Pokagon, the Potawatomi leader, protested the way Indians were presented at the Fair with his eloquent *Red Man's Greeting*, which was printed on birch bark and distributed on the Midway. An original birch bark printing of this, which includes a biographical sketch of Pokagon by his friend and publisher, C.H. Engle, is available for viewing at the Newberry Library, Special Collections (21). · The text of the *Red Man's Greeting* is also reprinted in Charles S. Winslow, *Indians of the Chicago Region* (29). Other writings by Simon Pokagon include a translation of the Lord's Prayer into Potawatomi (41); "The Future of the Red Man," an article about the World's Fair Indian School exhibit originally written for *Forum* in 1897, and reprinted in Bernd Peyer, *The Elders Wrote* (22); and the novel *Queen of the Woods*, which also includes a biographical sketch of Pokagon by Engle (23).

From September 26 through October 1, 1903, when Chicago celebrated its first centennial (the second celebration occurred in 1933, the hundredth anniversary of the actual incorporation of Chicago as a town) another Indian encampment was brought to the city. This was highly popular with the non-Indian public, judging by the newspaper coverage of the event. John McCutcheon, the well-known *Tribune* cartoonist, created a series of woodcuts of the celebration which were printed on the first page of the newspaper each day of that week. Nearly all of them included depictions of Indian participants or of the Indian Village in stereotypical terms, as symbols of savagery.

Numerous newspaper articles described the arrival and activities of the village and village members. Photocopies of many of these articles and of the McCutcheon wood-cuts are held in the clipping files of the Community Archives of NAES College; the newspapers are also on microfilm, available at numerous libraries.

The Chicago Centennial Commission published a 16 page guide to the Indian Village written by Edward B. Clark, and called *Indian Encampment At Lincoln Park, Chicago, Sept. 26 to Oct. 1, 1903, In Honor of the City's Centennial Anniversary* (40). This guide describes the six tribes represented at the encampment, prints a schedule of events, and also describes the re-enactment of the battle at Fort Dearborn, which Clark argues should *not* be called a massacre.

Other encampments were held in conjunction with Indian Day and

Indian Week celebrations at the end of each September beginning in 1919 and continuing at least through the early 1920s. These too are described, generally in stereotypical terms, in newspaper articles, copies of which are held in the clipfiles of the Community Archives of NAES College. Posters, pamphlets, and programs of these events are available at the Chicago Historical Society Graphics Collection and in the Chicago Historical Society Manuscript Collections' Welfare Council (48) and Indian Fellowship League collections (47).

Not only did Indians visit Chicago in the early 1900s, however; a few hundred Indians also lived here. The most famous Indian resident of Chicago in this period was Dr. Carlos Montezuma, a full-blood Yavapai who was kidnapped by Pimas at age four and then adopted by a white man. Montezuma grew up in a white world, but retained an Indian identity and fought for Indian rights. He worked his way through Chicago Medical School and, after a number of years as a physician at Indian Service schools, moved to Chicago. He practiced medicine here from the late 1890s until just prior to his death in 1923, when he returned to the Fort McDowell reservation to die and be buried.

Montezuma, a strong believer in assimilation, made it his life's project to attempt to eradicate the federal Indian Service or Indian Bureau (which became the Bureau of Indian Affairs (BIA) in 1947). He believed the Indian Bureau kept Indians oppressed and deprived Indians of the opportunity to advance in American society. So when a 1904 train wreck near Maywood killed three and injured fifteen Indian members of the Buffalo Bill Wild West Show, Montezuma not only treated the Indian survivors, but also pled on their behalf for fair compensation from the railroad company. His plea failed; the Indian Bureau accepted the settlement recommended by the Pine Ridge federal Indian agent, whose brother worked for the Buffalo Bill show.

In 1909 Montezuma helped found the Society of American Indians (SAI), a national pan-Indian organization. Some of the history of the SAI is described in Hazel W. Hertzberg, *The Search for an American Indian Identity, Modern Pan-Indian Movements* (17). The SAI was not radical enough for Montezuma; he intermittently broke with the group and rejoined it. He was especially active writing anti-Indian Bureau articles such as "Let My People Go" in the SAI's publication, *The Quarterly Journal* (33).

In 1916, frustrated with his limited role in the SAI, Montezuma founded a newspaper, *Wassaja*, published in Chicago (34). (Wassaja, Montezuma's Indian name, means signalling.) *Wassaja's* sole purpose was to encourage the abolition of the Indian Bureau. A biography of Carlos Montezuma's life, which unfortunately tells little about Montezuma's activities in Chicago, is Peter Iverson, *Carlos*

Montezuma and the Changing World of American Indians (20). The best sources for learning about Montezuma's activities in Chicago (which included greeting Indian delegations travelling between various reservations and Washington D.C., aiding Indians stranded in the city, and helping individuals find work) are the microfilm sets of the Carlos Montezuma papers, both available at the Newberry Library (31, 32).

Beginning in 1919 with the founding of the Indian Fellowship League, and especially with the founding of the Grand Council Fire of American Indians (now the Indian Council Fire) which occurred after Montezuma's death in 1923, organizations rather than individuals took the lead in providing services to Indians in Chicago.

The Indian Fellowship League, founded in 1919 and welcoming both Indian and white members, began with the purpose to educate Chicagoans about American Indians. The Fellowship League sponsored the popular encampments which annually drew tens of thousands, possibly over a hundred thousand, observers to the forest preserves in the early 1920s. By 1923, however, the Fellowship League had been accused of fostering negative stereotypes of Indians to make encampments popular, and the League did *not* sponsor the 1923 encampment. Information on the Fellowship League is available in the Chicago Historical Society Manuscript Collection (Indian Fellowship League folder) (47) and the Community Archives of NAES College (36, 49).

The Council Fire began in 1923 as a social and social service agency, although this function was not part of its stated purpose. Like the Fellowship League, its membership was Indian and white, and one of its major goals was educating the non-Indian public about Indians. Early annual reports indicate that the Council Fire provided financial aid to individual Indians and organized social activities for Indians in Chicago. As part of its educational function, the Council Fire in 1927 presented a resolution, calling for fair treatment of Indians by history books, to Mayor William Hale Thomson. This resolution, which lists Indian heroes and discusses "facts history books do not tell," was read into the U.S. *Congressional Record* on May 11, 1928 (30). A photocopy is available at the Community Archives of NAES College.

In 1933, at the Century of Progress World's Fair, the Council Fire presented its first annual Indian Achievement Award, to Dr. Charles A. Eastman, the Santee Sioux physician. The next year, at the 1934 Fair, the award was presented to Maria Martinez, the San Ildefonso Pueblo potter. In the 1950s, with the founding of the American Indian Center, which took over social service functions within the Indian community, the Council Fire voted to make the granting of the

Achievement Award its primary function. *The Indian Achievement Award of the Indian Council Fire*, compiled by Lola H. Hill, provides an historical sketch of the origins of the award, and biographies of award winners from the first fifty years (18). Discussion of the purposes of the Council Fire and its founding in 1923 is on pages 231-233 in Hertzberg, *The Search for an American Indian Identity* (17).

The documentary evidence of Indians in Chicago in the 1930s and 1940s remains sparse. The 1933-34 Century of Progress World's Fair and the 1948-49 Railroad Fair both sponsored Indian villages. The Century of Progress village was set up by promoters, and the Railroad Fair village was sponsored by the Santa Fe Railroad. This contrasts to the 1893 Fair's Indian village, which was created by ethnologists and the U.S. government. The purpose of the Indian villages at these later fairs was to provide entertainment and to show a way of life that was part of America's past. The purpose was no longer to show the stages of evolution of mankind.

As part of the Council Fire's participation in the 1933 Fair, an "Indian Hall of Honor" exhibit was erected. From this exhibit came Marion Gridley's famous book *Indians of Today*, which was published in 1936, and then revised in 1947, 1960, and 1971 (11, 12, 13, 14). The four editions of *Indians of Today* contain biographies of hundreds of important living Indians from throughout the United States. These books are rare; all four can be found at the State Historical Society of Wisconsin, but to find them all in Chicago, the reader must travel to several repositories.

Another source for some of the pre-World War II history of Indians in Chicago is the Chicago American Indian Oral History Project sponsored in 1983 by NAES College and the Newberry Library. Twenty-four community elders discussed their and their families' experiences in Chicago, from the 1930s or '40s or '50s through the 1980s. Donald L. Fixico, with the assistance of Lucille St. Germaine, has prepared a narrative entitled *Native Voices in the City* based on this project. This text, which provides invaluable insight into recent history of Chicago's Indian community, is nearing publication (8). Transcripts of the oral history interviews are available at the NAES College Library and the Newberry Library (38).

In the early 1950s the federal government began a relocation program, which is described in the article by Donald Fixico in this volume (Chapter 6). Relocation and non-government-sponsored migration by individual Indians to the city in search of work swelled the population of American Indians in Chicago into the thousands. Chicago's American Indian population has always been difficult to count for a number of reasons, five of which are enumerated in Bryan Marozas' *Demographic Profile of Chicago's American Indian Community* (42).

These reasons include high mobility of the Indian population, questions of self-identification, and fear and mistrust of the federal government based on past treatment of Indians by the bureaucracy.

The Oral History Project provides a view of Relocation from an Indian perspective (38). Newspaper articles show the reaction of Chicago's larger community to relocation; many of these can be read in the City Hall Municipal Reference Library, whose clip- files are arranged chronologically (37). A study of relocation which includes a case study of Chicago is Elaine M. Neils, *From Reservation to City, Indian Migration and Federal Relocation*, a University of Chicago Department of Geography Research Paper (43).

In response to Chicago's growing Indian population, American Indians founded the All-Tribes American Indian Center in 1953. The "All-Tribes" part of the title was important to its founders: it symbolically welcomed *all* Indians. (Members of approximately 100 different tribes live in Chicago today.) In 1955 the Center incorporated as the American Indian Center, which is its present title. From the beginning the Indian Center, as had the Council Fire, filled social and social service functions within the community. It differed from the Council Fire in the scope of its activities (Chicago's Indian population by the mid-1950s was much larger) and also because it acquired its own building on Wilson Avenue in Uptown in 1967. Chicago's Indian Center was the first of its kind in the United States; as such it served as a model for urban Indian Centers elsewhere. Merwyn S. Garbarino described "The Chicago American Indian Center: Two Decades" in Jack O. Waddell and O. Michael Watson, editors, *American Indian Urbanization* (9). Numerous newspaper articles discuss Indian Center activities, conflicts, and growth. These are described in David Beck, *The Chicago American Indian Community, 1893-1988, Annotated Bibliography and Guide to Sources in Chicago*, listing numbers 651-735 (2). Many are available in the various clip files: at the City Hall Municipal Reference Library (37), at the Chicago Historical Society (35), or in the Community Archives of NAES College (36). A large amount of Indian Center documents are contained in both the Community Archives of NAES College and the Chicago Historical Society Manuscript Collections Church Federation of Greater Chicago papers (46).

By 1961 American Indians were fed up with the federal policies of relocation and termination. From June 13-20, 1961, an historic conference, the American Indian Chicago Conference (AICC) convened at the University of Chicago. The AICC, originated by University of Chicago anthropologist Sol Tax, was organized by Indian leaders from throughout the United States. The concrete result of this conference was *The Declaration of Indian Purpose*, a statement of Indian goals and needs written by Indians (28). The 1961 AICC is generally viewed as a landmark symbol of the Indian right to choose an Indian future, and as a turning point in Indian participation in political processes. Numerous sources describe the AICC; see listing numbers 2016-2047 in Beck's *Bibliography* (2). The importance of the AICC extends far beyond the conference itself: for instance, a work that looks at Indian issues in the 1980s and toward the 21st century, *New Directions in Indian Purpose*, edited by Terry Straus, is subtitled *Reflections on the American Indian Chicago Conference* (26). The conference reported in this book was a twenty-fifth anniversary response to the AICC.

In the late 1960s Maria Tallchief, the world-renowned Osage ballerina and winner of the 1967 Council Fire Achievement Award, retired from dancing and moved to Chicago. Two biographies of her, written for children, are Marion E. Gridley, *Maria Tallchief, the Story of an Indian Woman* (15) and Adele DeLeeuw, *Maria Tallchief, American Ballerina* (4).

The 1960s and 1970s saw a proliferation of Indian agencies in Chicago. St. Augustine's Center for American Indians was founded in 1961 as a social service agency to meet the needs of Indians not helped by the Indian Center. Other organizations grew later in the 1960s and early 1970s out of activist groups. Native American Committee (NAC) is an example. Organizations formed to meet increasingly specialized needs, such as health, employment, and education. Information on many of these organizations and agencies, including documents and newspaper articles, is available in the Community Archives of NAES College (49). *The American Indian Community Service Directory* lists and describes presently active organizations and agencies (39).

In 1981 the agencies within the Indian community met in an attempt to overcome differences and work toward common goals. CAICOC (Chicago American Indian Community Organizations Conference) was thus founded; it remains important within the Indian community today. CAICOC's *Statement of Purpose*, edited by Robert Archiquette and Louis Delgado, was published in 1981 (1). Following this, CAICOC initiated action plans to deal with the problems and issues it defined as important to Chicago's Indian community. Articles and documents relating to CAICOC are also available at the Community Archives of NAES College (49).

In the early 1980s the Newberry Library sponsored a project, "Seeing Indian in Chicago," which collected photographs of Chicago's Indian community for display (45). This collection is now housed at the Newberry Library. In another project, Portraits of Indian Chicago, A Hall of Honor, four Indian artists in Chicago painted portraits of Indian leaders in Chicago (44). Some of these portraits are on display in NAES College, and others remain in the keeping of the Chicago Indian Artists' Guild. A movie based on this project, "Portraits of Indian Chicago," made for public television, is in the NAES College Library videotape collection.

The history of urban American Indians in Chicago in the twentieth century is rich and varied. Many sources that lead us to a better understanding of this community exist. These sources include conventional writings such as books and articles, and harder to find sources such as personal papers, documents, and visual material including posters and paintings and photographs. The deeper we look into these sources, the more we discover is in them—and the more sources we discover exist.

Sources

Books

1. Robert Archiquette and Louis Delgado, eds., *Chicago American Indian Community Organizations Conference Statement of Purpose* (Chicago: NAES College Press, 1981). Available at the NAES College Library and the NAES College Bookstore.

2. David Beck, *The Chicago American Indian Community, 1893-1988, Annotated Bibliography and Guide to Sources in Chicago* (Chicago: NAES College Press, 1988). Distributed by Chicago Academy Press.

3. *Declaration of Indian Purpose*. AICC. See *The Voice of the American Indian*, below.

4. Adele DeLeeuw, *Maria Tallchief, American Ballerina* (Champaign: Garrand Publishing Company, 1971).

5. Department of Publicity and Promotion, M. P. Handy, Chief, ed., *World's Columbian Exposition 1893 Official Catalogue, Part XII, Anthropological Building, Midway Plaisance, and Isolated Exhibits, Department M, Ethnology, Archaeology, Physical Anthropology, History, Natural History, Isolated Collected Exhibits, F. W. Putnam, Chief* (Chicago: W. B. Conkey Company, 1893). 84 pp. Part of Official Catalogue, which contains all volumes. At Chicago Historical Society.

6. Ex-Governor William E. Cameron of the World's Columbian Exposition History Co., with an Introduction by Hon. Thomas W. Palmer, *The World's Fair, Being a Pictorial History of the Columbian Exposition Containing a Complete History of the World- Renowned Exposition at Chicago, Captivating Descriptions of the Magnificent Buildings and Marvelous Exhibits, Such as Works of Art, Textile Fabrics, Machinery, Natural Products, the Latest Inventions, Discoveries, Etc., Etc., with A Description of Chicago, its Wonderful Buildings, Parks, Etc.* (Chicago: Chicago Publication and Lithograph Co., 1893). At Chicago Historical Society.

7. *Felix S. Cohen's Handbook of Federal Indian Law* (Albuquerque: University of New Mexico Press, [1942]).

8. Donald L. Fixico, with the assistance of Lucille St. Germaine, *Native Voices in the City: The Chicago American Indian Oral History Project*. Awaiting publication. Manuscript available in Community Archives of NAES College.

9. Merqyn S. Garbarino, "The Chicago American Indian Center: Two Decades" in Jack O. Waddell and O. Michael Watson, editors, *American*

Indian Urbanization (Institute for the Study of Social Change, Department of Sociology and Anthropology, Purdue University Institute Monograph Series, Number 4, 1973).

10. D. Getches and C. Wilkinson, *Federal Indian Law: Cases and Materials* (St. Paul, Minnesota. West Publishing Co., 1986).

11. Marion Gridley, *Indians of Today* (Chicago: Indian Council Fire, 1936). Available at the Library of the Field Museum of Natural History and the Newberry Library.

12. Marion Gridley, *Indians of Today*, 2nd edition (Chicago: Millar Publishing Co., 1947). Available at Northwestern University Library and the Newberry Library.

13. Marion Gridley, *Indians of Today*, 3rd edition (Chicago: Towertown Press, 1960). Available at NAES College Library.

14. Marion Gridley, *Indians of Today*, 4th edition (USA: ICFP, Inc., 1971). Available at Northwestern University Library.

15. Marion Gridley, *Maria Tallchief, the Story of an Indian Woman* (Minneapolis: Dillon Press, Inc., 1973).

16. Moses P. Handy, Chief of the Department of Publicity and Editor, *The Official Directory of the World's Columbian Exposition May 1st to October 30th, 1893, A Reference Book...* copiously illustrated (Chicago: W. B. Conkey Company, 1893). At Chicago Historical Society.

17. Hazel W. Hertzberg, *The Search for an American Indian Identity, Modern Pan-Indian Movements* (Syracuse: Syracuse University Press, 1971).

18. Lola H. Hill, ed., *The Indian Achievement Award of the Indian Council Fire*, (Chicago: Indian Council Fire, 1982). Available at the NAES College Library.

19. *The Historical World's Columbian Exposition and Chicago Guide...*, illustrated from official drawings by Horace H. Morgan, LL. D. (St. Louis: James H. Mason & Co., Publishers [c. 1893]). At Chicago Historical Society.

20. Peter Iverson, *Carlos Montezuma and the Changing World of American Indians* (Albuquerque: University of New Mexico Press, 1982).

21. Chief Pokagon, *Red Man's Greeting* (Hartford, Michigan: C.H. Engle, publisher, 1893). An original, printed on birch bark, available at the Newberry Library, Special Collections.

22. Simon Pokagon, "The Future of the Red Man," reprinted in Bernd Peyer, *The Elders Wrote* (Berlin: Dietrich Reimer Verlag, 1982). Available at the NAES College Library and NAES College bookstore.

23. Simon Pokagon, *O-Gi-Maw-Kwe Mit-I-Gwa-Ki (Queen of the Woods)* (Hartford, Michigan: C.H. Engle, publisher, 1899). Available in the Newberry Library, Special Collections.

24. Robert W. Rydell, *All the World's a Fair, Visions of Empire at American International Expositions, 1876-1916* (Chicago: University of Chicago Press, 1984).

25. Edward H. Spicer, "American Indians, Federal Policy Toward," pp. 114-122 in Stephan Thernstrom, ed., *Harvard Encyclopedia of American Ethnic Groups* (Cambridge, Mass.: Belknap Press, 1980).

26. Terry Straus, ed., *New Directions in Indian Purpose: Reflections on the American Indian Chicago Conference.* (Chicago: NAES College Press, 1988).

27. Russell E. Thornton, Gary D. Sandefur, and Harold G. Grasmick, *The Urbanization of American Indians, A Critical Bibliography,* The Newberry Library Center for the History of the American Indian Bibliographical Series, Francis Jennings, General Editor, William R. Swagerty, Assistant Editor (Bloomington: Indiana University Press, 1982).

28. *The Voice of the American Indian, Declaration of Indian Purpose* (Chicago: American Indian Chicago Conference, The University of Chicago, June 13-20, 1961).

29. Charles S. Winslow, *Indians of the Chicago Region* (Chicago: Soderlund Printing Service/Charles S. Winslow, Publisher, 1946). Available at the Chicago Historical Society Library, the Chicago Public Library, and the Newberry Library, Special Collections.

Government Document

30. *Congressional Record*, Volume 69, Part VIII; 70th Congress, 1st Session; May 11, 1928; pp. 8369-8370.

Microfilm

31. *The Carlos Montezuma Papers* (State Historical Society of Wisconsin Collection, 1974). This is a film of the collection of the State Historical Society of Wisconsin. Available at the Newberry Library.

32. *The Papers of Carlos Montezuma, M.D., Including the Papers of Maria Keller Montezuma Moore and the Papers of Joseph W. Latimer,* edited by John William Larner, Jr. (Wilmington, Delaware: Scholarly Resources, Inc., 1983). This set contains documents from forty repositories and sixty newspapers. Available at the Newberry Library.

Photocopies of selected documents from the Wisconsin collection are held in the Community Archives of NAES College.

Newspapers and Journals

33. *The Quarterly Journal of the Society of American Indians.* Available in the Newberry Library, Special Collections.

34. *Wassaja,* Carlos Montezuma's monthly newspaper, published in Chicago from 1916 through 1923. Copies of *Wassaja,* which Montezuma published until his death, are available in the two microfilm sets of Carlos Montezuma's papers held at the Newberry Library. Photocopies made from sixteen of the forty two issues of *Wassaja* held at the State Historical Society of Wisconsin are available at the Community Archives of NAES College.

Newspaper Clipfile Collections

35. Chicago Historical Society Library clipfiles. Social Service Agencies. American Indian Center.

36. Community Archives of NAES College clipfiles.

37. Municipal Reference Library of Chicago clipfiles: Ethnic Groups, Chicago, Indians, American.

Oral History

38. Chicago American Indian Oral History Project. Transcripts of the 23 interviews of community elders are available at the Newberry Library and the NAES College Library. Tapes of the interviews are available at NAES College Library. Restricted use.

Pamphlets, Etc.

39. *American Indian Community Service Directory* (Chicago: Information and Assistance Center, NAES College). Available at the NAES College Library and the NAES College Bookstore.

40. Edward B. Clark, *Indian Encampment At Lincoln Park, Chicago, Sept. 26 to Oct. 1, 1903, In Honor of the City's Centennial Anniversary* (Chicago: Faithorn Printing Company). Available at Chicago Historical Society Library.

41. The Lord's Prayer, translated into Potawatomi, printed on birch bark, 6" x 3 1/2". Available in Chicago Historical Society Graphics Collection.

Reports

42. Bryan Marozas, *Demographic Profile of Chicago's American Indian Community* (Chicago: NAES College Information and Assistance Center, 1984). Available at the NAES College Library and the NAES College Bookstore.

43. Elaine M. Neils, *From Reservation to City, Indian Migration and Federal Relocation*, (Chicago: The University of Chicago Department of Geography Research Paper, Number 131, 1971).

Visual Resources

44. Portraits of Indian Chicago, A Hall of Honor. Four Indian artists in Chicago painted portraits of Indian leaders in Chicago. Some of these portraits are on display in NAES College, others are in the keeping of the Chicago Indian Artists' Guild, and others remain pending. A film, "Portraits of Indian Chicago," is available in the NAES College Library videotape collection.

45. "Seeing Indian in Chicago." This collection is now housed at the Newberry Library, where it is kept for Indian community use.

Manuscript Collections

46. Chicago Historical Society Manuscript Collections. Church Federation of Greater Chicago.

47. Chicago Historical Society Manuscript Collections. Indian Fellowship League Folder.

48. Chicago Historical Society Manuscript Collections. Welfare Council Box 246, folders 13 and 14.

49. Community Archives of NAES College organization and agency records.

ABOUT THE AUTHORS

Debra Anderson (Chippewa) is a student at NAES/Chicago working toward a B.A. degree in Indian Community Studies.

David Beck, M.A., Archivist for NAES/Chicago is working on his Ph.D in History at the University of Illinois at Chicago, and is the author of the annotated bibliography, *The Chicago American Indian Community, 1893-1988.*

Violet Brown is Administrative Assistant at the McNickle Center for the History of the American Indian at Chicago's Newberry Library. She received her B.A. degree from NAES College/Chicago.

Brenda Snowball Carley received her B.A. degree in Community Studies from NAES College/Chicago. She is currently employed as Career Advisor by the American Indian Business Association in Chicago.

Vince Catches (Lakota) was awarded his B.A. in Community Studies from NAES College/Chicago.

Donald L. Fixico, Ph.D., of Indian heritage from Oklahoma, is Associate Professor of History at the University of Wisconsin- Milwaukee. Dr. Fixico is the author of several articles primarily on federal-Indian relations in the twentieth century, and authored the book, *Termination and Relocation: Federal Indian Policy, 1945-1960 (1986).*

Sarah Gallagher (Sioux) is a student at NAES/Chicago working toward a B.A. in Indian Community Studies.

Lincus Harris received his B.A. in Community Studies from NAES College/Chicago.

Rosalyn LaPier (Blackfeet), B.A., is Director of the Library and Resource Center at NAES/Chicago. She is currently a student at DePaul working toward an M.A. in Liberal Studies.

Nora Lloyd (Chippewa) is a student at NAES/Chicago working toward a B.A. in Indian Community Studies.

Chris Migwans (Ojibwa) is a student at NAES/Chicago.

Jay Miller (Delaware), Ph.D., is Assistant Director of the D'Arcy McNickle Center for the History of the American Indian.

Yvonne Murry (Ojibwa) is Director of the American Indian Economic Development Association in Chicago. She is currently working toward a B.A. in Indian Community Studies at NAES/Chicago.

Frances Oshkenaniew (Menominee) is a student at NAES/Menominee.

Christine Red Cloud (Chippewa) is a student at NAES/Chicago and is employed at NAES in the Office of the President.

Margaret Red Cloud (Chippewa) is a student at NAES/Chicago and is the Social Service Coordinator at the American Indian Center.

Terry Straus, Ph.D., is Senior Resident Faculty at NAES/Chicago, responsible for the core curriculum at that campus.

Helen Tanner received her Ph.D. in History from the University of Michigan, is a Research Associate at the Newberry Library. She has written extensively in the field of Indian Studies and is author of *Atlas of Great Lakes Indian History*.

Virgil Vogel received his Ph.D. from the University of Chicago, and is a retired professor from the Social Science Department, Truman College, City Colleges of Chicago. He has written several books, including *This Country Was Ours, American Indian Medicine, American Indian Place Names in Illinois,* and *Indian Place Names in Michigan,* and many articles on American Indian History.

Dorene Wiese (Chippewa), M.A., is the Dean of Administration at Truman College, City Colleges of Chicago.